Happy

Lots of

Annie xx

and Pierre ☺

ALL ABOUT
SOUPS & STEWS

ALL ABOUT
SOUPS & STEWS

IRMA S. ROMBAUER
MARION ROMBAUER BECKER
ETHAN BECKER

PHOTOGRAPHY BY TUCKER & HOSSLER

A Dorling Kindersley Book

Dorling [DK] Kindersley

LONDON, NEW YORK, SYDNEY, DELHI, PARIS, MUNICH AND JOHANNESBURG

First published in Great Britain in 2001 by
Dorling Kindersley Limited, 9 Henrietta Street, London WC2E 8PS

Published by arrangement with the original publisher,
Scribner, an imprint of Simon & Schuster, Inc.

Joy of Cooking All About series was designed
and produced by Weldon Owen Inc.,
814 Montgomery Street, San Francisco,
California 94133, USA

Set in Joanna MT and Gill Sans

Reproduced by Bright Arts Singapore
Text film output by Mick Hodson Associates
Printed in Singapore by Tien Wah Press (Pte.) Ltd.

A CIP catalogue record for this book is available from
The British Library

ISBN 0 7513 3534 7

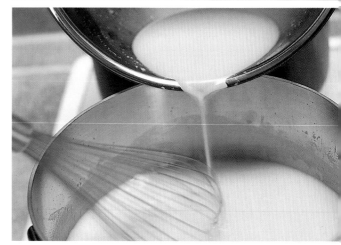

NOTE: Use either metric or imperial measurements since
conversions are not exact equivalents.

see our complete catalogue at
www.dk.com

Recipe shown on half-title page: *New York Deli Borscht*, 48
Recipe shown on title page: *Fresh Tomato Soup*, 51

CONTENTS

FOREWORD

"Making the pot smile." My Granny Rom and my mother enjoyed quoting the English translation of the French phrase in early editions of the Joy of Cooking to describe the gentle simmering required for soups and stews. Soups and stews have the power to bring smiles not just to the pot but also to the people who eat them.

That's why an entire volume of the new All About series is devoted to soups and stews. All About Soups & Stews offers information on key ingredients, along with recipes for a wide variety of stocks, embellishments and accompanying breads – everything you need whether you're just starting dinner with soup or making a robust stew the centrepiece of your meal.

You might notice that this collection of kitchen-tested recipes is adapted from the latest edition of the Joy of Cooking. Just as our family has done for generations, we have worked to make this version of Joy a little bit better than the last. As a result, you'll find that some notes, recipes and techniques have been changed to improve their clarity and usefulness. Since 1931, the Joy of Cooking has constantly evolved. And now, the All About series has taken Joy to a whole new stage, as you will see from the beautiful colour photographs of finished dishes and clearly illustrated instructions for preparing and serving them. Granny Rom and Mother would have been delighted.

I'm sure you'll find All About Soups & Stews to be both a useful and an enduring companion in your kitchen.

Enjoy!

Ethan Becker pictured with his grandmother, Irma von Starkloff Rombauer (left), and his mother, Marion Rombauer Becker (right). Irma Rombauer published the first Joy of Cooking *at her own expense in 1931. Marion Rombauer Becker became coauthor in 1951.* Joy *as it has progressed through the decades (from top left to bottom right): the 1931 edition with Marion's depiction of St. Martha of Bethany, said to be the patron saint of cooking, "slaying the dragon of kitchen drudgery"; the 1943 edition; the 1951 edition; the 1962 edition; the 1975 edition; and the 1997 edition.*

About Soups & Stews

If any foods seem inherently calming, and even consoling, they are soup and stew. Soups and stews feel good when the weather gets cold. They restore our spirit and our vigour. (The first "restaurants" were eighteenth-century Parisian establishments that served rich soups to restore, or *restaurer*, the hungry citizenry.) In the old days, when a "soup batch" of vegetables and herbs cost a few pence and bones were free from the local butcher, home cooks routinely made soups from scratch. Today, the smell of a wonderful soup or a hearty stew simmering on the stove in the kitchen still symbolizes home cooking.

Tools for Making Stocks, Soups and Stews

The basic tools for making stocks, soups and stews are a wooden spoon, a ladle, and, of course, a pot. An 8-10 litre (13-16 pint) pot (**1**) is required for making stock (see *About Stocks & Broths*, 13) or large batches of soup or stew. A 4-litre (6-pint) pot is about right for everyday use.

The best type is narrow, tall and heavy-bottomed, to allow the stock, soup or stew to simmer gently without too much evaporation and to facilitate skimming.

For making stock, just be sure the pot is large enough to accommodate all of the solids (bones, shells or vegetables) with room to cover them with 5cm (2in) of water. Flameproof casseroles (**2**) or wide soup pots also work, as long as you monitor the simmering stock and add more water whenever the level drops below the solids. Using an 8-10 litre (13-16 pint) stockpot will yield 2-4 litre (3¼ -6½ pint) batches of stock. Avoid aluminium pots, which may react with the ingredients and affect the flavour. A second large pot is handy for cooling strained stock; plastic containers work, but they insulate, and so the stock will not cool as quickly.

For making brown stocks, it is also essential to have a large roasting tin, preferably with handles. Sieves are another must – ideally two of them, one coarse and one fine. The long-handled conical kind, called a chinois or China cap (**3**), is ideal, but you can improvise a fine-mesh sieve by lining a colander with a double layer of muslin, a dampened layer of paper towels or a coffee filter. Gravy separators, also called fat separators, are a convenient way to remove excess fat from stock when there is no time to chill the stock and let the fat solidify.

Equipment for Making Soups

Some soups in this book are puréed to make them smooth; others are partially puréed to give them a "creamier" texture. Here are the pros and cons to using commonly available kitchen equipment to adjust the texture of a soup.

Food Processor: This tool is especially good for thick soups. Beware of overloading, as liquids can leak out the bottom or overflow. Depending on the size of your food processor, it may be best to purée soups in two batches. Or you can purée the solid ingredients with just enough liquid to keep the blade from clogging; return the purée to the pot, and stir or whisk to blend.

Blender (1): A blender works well for puréeing thinner soups. When blending hot soup, do not fill the blender more than one-third full. Wrap a tea towel around the lid and start on a low speed, then gradually increase the speed.

Hand-Held Immersion Blender (2): This tool is exceptionally convenient, because it is portable and easy to clean. Just immerse the blade end in the soup and turn it on, moving it around the soup until you achieve the desired texture. The solid ingredients must be very soft for the blender to work, and it can never create a completely silken texture. But the immersion blender is still an excellent tool for soups that are only partially puréed, such as some bean soups.

Food Mill (3): Once a soup is cooked until the ingredients are quite soft, the food mill purées and strains simultaneously. Interchangeable discs help the cook control the final texture of the soup. A food mill also strains out tomato seeds.

Making Substitutions

Soups and stews that begin by sautéing vegetables in oil or butter can be adapted by cutting the fat in half and adding 60ml (2floz) water or stock, which sweats the vegetables rather than sautés them. The same vegetables can also be cooked directly in the soup or stew liquid with no previous sautéing at all. Even if you are not concerned about fat, stock should always be degreased before use (see *About Stocks & Broths*, 13) for purely aesthetic reasons. If meat is cooked in a soup or stew, trim it thoroughly; after it has cooked, carefully ladle the fat from the surface – or refrigerate the soup or stew overnight so the fat rises to the top and solidifies, then carefully remove it from the surface.

Most recipes calling for cream can be made with less cream than specified or with none at all, but before you decide against a recipe calling for cream, divide the total amount of cream by the number of servings. Most of the time, a serving of the soup or stew will contain only a few tablespoons of cream. If the soup is not boiled, you can often substitute semi-skimmed milk, yoghurt or sour cream (which has half the fat of standard cream).

Using Pasta in Soups

Italy's pasta soups fall into two major categories: filled or other pastas cooked in stock and garnished only with grated cheese, and brothy home-style soups with tiny or broken pasta, vegetables or other flavourful ingredients.

Italian home cooks use whatever is to hand, boiling up broth and dropping into it whatever pasta is handy; by the time the pasta is tender, the vegetables are just right. For more substance, they beat together an egg or two with grated cheese and stir it into the soup about a minute before taking it off the stove.

Tiny pastas are used in several styles of soups: Cook them in the stock and finish the soup with chopped fresh herbs and/or grated cheese and/or beaten egg stirred in at the last moment. Add pasta with vegetables or other ingredients for brothy soups.

- Small shapes: meloni, orzo, pastine, tubetti, ditalini, anellini (little rings), stelline, avene (oats), tempestine and quadrettini.
- Break these long strands into clear soups to whatever size you need: pappardelle, lasagnette, maltagliati, lasagne, bucatini, capellini, vermicelli, spaghetti and linguine.

STORING SOUPS AND STEWS

Soups and stews keep well, tightly covered in the refrigerator, improving in flavour. The exception is a recipe made with fish and seafood. The delicate flavours of the fish are best as soon as they are cooked. Fruit soups and soups and stews made with meat, poultry, milk, cream or eggs keep for up to 3 days. Those made of vegetables and pulses keep for up to 4 days.

Refrigerate soup or stew when it has completely cooled and cover tightly. Always store in a container that it completely fills – air is the enemy. For the same reason, be sure to leave any fat on top until serving time, as the layer seals the soup or stew beneath.

All soups and stews can be frozen. Soups that contain chunks of vegetables that do not freeze well – root vegetables, for example – can be puréed after thawing, then heated with enough stock or milk to loosen. Puréed soups hold their quality for up to 3 months in the freezer. Stews and other soups are best served within 1 month of freezing.

SERVING SOUPS AND STEWS

You can serve soup or stew in anything that will hold it, but over the centuries certain bowls have become traditional for certain soups and stews.

First-course soups are usually presented in smaller bowls (**1**) than hearty main-course stews.

Cream soups and consommés, which cool quickly, are traditionally served in comparatively deep bowls (**2**). Occasionally an elegant broth is served in actual demitasse cups and sipped like espresso. The bowls of cream-soup spoons are deep and nearly rounded so that they can hold a reasonable quantity of liquid.

Stews, chowders, fish soups and other soups with numerous ingredients, which are slower to cool, are usually served in shallow, broad-rimmed dishes (**3**) or in underplates; the appropriate spoons are long-handled and have shallow oval-shaped bowls (**4**) that can hold plenty of chunks.

Use ovenproof bowls or crocks (**5**) for a soup such as French onion, which requires time in the oven.

If you can, serve Oriental soups in Chinese or Japanese lacquer or ceramic bowls with those distinctive open-handled ceramic Oriental soup spoons (**6**).

As for serving size, consider 250ml (8floz) of soup as a first course and 375 to 500ml (12 to 16floz) of soup or stew as a main course.

ABOUT **STOCKS** & BROTHS

*S*tocks and broths are a vital ingredient in many soups and stews, and no shop-bought variety can compare with a well-tended homemade version. Stock making is different from other kinds of cooking. Instead of calling for tender, young ingredients, stocks are best made with meat from older animals and mature vegetables, cooked slowly for a long time to extract every vestige of flavour. Purists may insist on using only fish stock in a fish soup or beef stock in a beef stew, but today's household rarely has the luxury of such precision. Since chicken and vegetable stocks are the mildest in flavour and the easiest to prepare, they have become our most popular – and can be used for, among other things, both fish soup and beef stew if necessary. Certainly, full-flavoured beef stock or savoury white veal stock is still worth making if you have the time.

Clockwise from top: *Vegetable Stock, 20; Chicken Stock, 22; Brown Beef Stock, 24*

13

Making Stocks and Broths

The characteristics of any good stock are flavour, body and clarity. Of the three, flavour is paramount, and the way to get it is by using a high proportion of ingredients to water. The most flavourful stocks are made with only enough water to cover the bones, shells or vegetables. Additional water is needed only when it evaporates below the level of the ingredients before the stock is fully cooked. Follow the recipes for ideal ratios of liquid to solids, but the principle is simple: keep the solids covered while cooking.

Cooking times for stocks depend on how long it takes to extract all the flavour from the ingredients. While it takes at least 8 hours for raw beef bones to give up all their richness and flavour, chicken bones only need to be boiled for half that time. Vegetable and fish stocks rarely require more than an hour to cook. In fact, their delicate flavours will deteriorate if overcooked. When preparing ingredients for stock making, it is important to chop vegetables and bones to size according to their cooking times – large for long cooking and small for quick cooking – to allow their flavours to be fully extracted.

Simmering the stock past the recipe's recommended cooking time can produce an unpleasant bitter taste. A stock should be strained when all the flavours and goodness have been fully extracted from the meat, bones and vegetables. If in doubt, retrieve a meaty bone from the simmering stock. If the meat still has some flavour, allow the stock to simmer for longer. If the meat is entirely tasteless and the bone joints are falling apart, it is time to strain the stock.

If a stock tastes weak after straining, remove and discard the fat, then simmer the stock briskly to reduce the water content and concentrate the flavour. This technique, known as reduction and used extensively in sauce making, does produce a more deeply flavoured stock, but in the process much of the aromatic, fresh taste of the vegetables is lost. For this reason, we do not recommend reducing vegetable stock. In addition, not all dishes require a deep, concentrated flavour. A light stock is sometimes more appropriate for its subtlety. In instances when you want a hearty stock, first roast the bones and vegetables in a hot oven. Then transfer the bones and vegetables to the stockpot, pour off any excess grease, and add water or wine to the hot roasting tin to release the intensely flavoured caramelized cooking juices – a step known as deglazing. Add the liquid to the stockpot. The resulting brown stock is darker and richer than a stock made by straight simmering, which is referred to as a white stock. This technique can be used for meat, poultry, fish or vegetable stocks.

When choosing meat or bones for the stockpot, understand that meat adds flavour, while bones contribute body. Bones, especially those from the joints (knuckles and shoulders) of young animals, contain gelatin, which gives a stock body and a rich, smooth texture. Always use a combination of bones and meat, or look for particularly meaty bones. By definition, a stock is made with more bones than meat,

while a broth is made from meat. For economy's sake, meat or poultry used for stock making can be removed from the pot before the stock is ready (while the meat still has flavour) and reserved for another meal; see *Express Chicken Broth*, 29. The resulting light stock can be used as is, or the bones can be returned to the pot and the stock cooked further. Raw ingredients produce the best stock, but at a pinch, leftover meat or vegetables will do. Leftover carcasses, such as turkey, broken up and pushed under the water, make a fine stock.

The clarity of a stock is more than an aesthetic concern. A clear stock tastes clean and fresh, while a cloudy one will often seem greasy and muddled. The secret to a clear stock is to start with cold water, allow it to come slowly to a boil, then immediately lower the temperature to the slightest simmer while you carefully skim any impurities, froth, or fat that rises to the surface. This technique not only brings the most flavour out of the ingredients but also draws out impurities in the meat and bones that would otherwise cloud your stock. If a stock is permitted to boil, these impurities, in the form of the scum that forms on the surface of the stock, will be incorporated into the liquid instead. If you do not have enough time to simmer a stock gently, consider preparing one of the express broth recipes in this section. Some are made from scratch, and some call for doctoring already-prepared ingredients. All are time savers.

ADAPTING FLAVOUR

If you prefer a lighter soup or a vegetarian soup, any of the all-vegetable stocks, 20, or *Vegetable Broth*, 29, can replace a meat, poultry, fish or seafood stock in soups and stews. When you need a substitute for beef stock, it is worth your time to prepare *Roast Vegetable Stock*, 20, which has a similar depth of flavour. Remember that no matter what the soup, a small quantity of salt pork, a ham bone or a few slices of bacon will add depth in a short time. Use these and other robustly flavoured ingredients sparingly. It takes just a little to flavour the pot. Ingredients such as these should not overwhelm the other ingredients, but should be used to enrich flavour.

RULES FOR MAKING STOCKS AND BROTHS

• Cut the ingredients into small pieces for quick-cooking stocks and broths, and larger pieces for long-cooking stocks (**1**). Express broths use the smallest-cut ingredients, followed by fish stock, then vegetable stock, then poultry and lastly meat.

• The higher the ratio of solids to water, the more flavourful the stock or broth. The water should just barely cover the ingredients (**2**). Add water during cooking if necessary.

• Start with cold water and bring it slowly to a simmer. Never rush a stock. Simmer gently so bubbles just barely break on the surface.

• Never allow a stock to boil.

• Skim the impurities that rise to the surface as the stock or broth simmers – often during the first 30 minutes, and then once an hour or so (**3**). Have two bowls nearby, one filled with water to set the skimmer in so that it does not get covered with congealed fat and impurities, and a second bowl to collect what you skim off.

• Adjust the flavour. If the stock tastes too thin, simmer it for longer. As the water evaporates, the stock reduces in volume and its flavour becomes concentrated. Vegetable stock is bitter when over-reduced.

• Stop cooking the stock when there is no flavour left in the ingredients.

• A well-made stock or broth contains very little fat. Begin by trimming all

meat and bones of visible fat, and finish by either skimming the stock or broth carefully while still warm or chilling it so the fat forms a solid layer and is easily removed (**4**). Alternatively, and easiest yet, use an inexpensive gravy separator (**5**).

• Many variables affect the yield of a stock or broth recipe, such as the size of the pot and the kind of meat or bones used. Ultimately, a good flavour is more important than achieving the exact yield.

Seasoning Stocks and Broths

Stocks and broths are usually meant to be comparatively unassertive in flavour so that they can be used for a number of purposes. Onions, carrots and celery, the traditional mixture of aromatic vegetables for stocks and broths, known as a mirepoix in French, should be added sparingly about 30 minutes after the stock has begun to simmer and the impurities have been removed.

Different styles of cooking alter this classic mixture; in some parts of America, for instance, the standard vegetable mixture includes onions, green peppers and celery. Mushrooms and leeks are also common. The discreet use of either fresh or dried seasonings, including parsley, thyme, bay leaves and peppercorns, in the form of a bouquet garni, is equally important.

For express broth or quick-cooking stocks, there is no need to tie the seasonings in a bundle – they can simply be tossed in with the vegetables. Salt is almost never added to stocks and broths. The reduction process, during both the original simmering and any subsequent cooking, would concentrate the salt and ruin the results. Vegetable stocks are an exception to the rule. Because they are lighter in flavour and are rarely reduced, some cooks add a small amount of salt during cooking to bring out the flavours.

Court Bouillon

1 litre (1 ½ pints)

Court bouillon is a seasoned liquid cooked for only a short time (court is French for short) and is especially useful when you haven't the time to make an actual stock or when a recipe for soup or stew requires only a lightly flavoured broth. The composition of a court bouillon can vary, but most contain some type of acid (lemon juice or wine vinegar) and an assortment of aromatic vegetables and herbs such as parsley, thyme and bay leaves. Court bouillon and Vegetable Stock, 20, are generally interchangeable, but vegetable stock has no lemon juice or vinegar.

Combine in a stockpot over medium heat:

1.5 litres (2½ pints) cold water
60g (2oz) chopped onions
60g (2oz) chopped celery
4 tbsp chopped leeks, tender white part only, washed thoroughly
4 tbsp chopped carrots
1 Bouquet Garni, right

Bring to a boil, reduce the heat and let simmer gently, uncovered, until the vegetables are tender, about 20 minutes. Add:

3 tbsp lemon juice or white wine vinegar

Simmer for another 10 minutes. Strain into a clean pot or heatproof plastic container. If desired, season with:

Salt and ground black pepper to taste

Use immediately to make soups or stews or let cool, uncovered, then refrigerate until ready to use.

Bouquet Garni

Since herbs tend to float and get in the way as you skim the surface of a stock, we recommend tying them together in a little packet, known as a bouquet garni. Vary the contents to suit your dish, with additions such as whole cloves, dill, lemon zest or garlic. For express broth or quick-cooking stocks, simply toss the seasonings in with the vegetables.

Wrap in a 10 × 10cm (4 × 4in) piece of muslin:

Small bunch of parsley or parsley stems
8 sprigs fresh thyme, or 1 tsp dried
1 bay leaf
2 or 3 celery leaves (optional)

Tie the muslin securely with a piece of kitchen string or omit the muslin and simply tie the herbs together at their stems.

Refrigerate in a tightly covered container until ready to use.

Reducing Stock to a Glaze

Meat, poultry and fish (but not vegetable) stocks can be cooked down, or reduced, until they become a thick, syrupy glaze that is both potent and delectable. Although the lengthy reduction takes patience and care, the end product becomes a wonderfully convenient "secret ingredient" for seasoning and finishing all manner of soups and stews. When it is fully reduced, a glaze is just 10 to 15 percent of the volume of original stock and will last for months tightly covered in the refrigerator. Reduced fish stock tends to be too strong for most tastes.
Prepare:

1 litre (1½ pints) *Brown Beef Stock, 24, Brown Veal Stock, 25, or Brown Chicken Stock, 22*

Degrease the stock well and place it in a large pot over medium-high heat. Allow the stock to simmer vigorously. Skim any foam that rises to the surface and transfer the stock to gradually smaller pots as it reduces in volume. Lower the heat when the stock begins to get noticeably thicker and more concentrated to avoid burning. The glaze is ready when it coats the back of a spoon and only about 250ml (8floz) remains, anywhere from 2 to 4 hours depending on the shape of the pan.

Remove from the heat and let cool. The glaze will solidify and feel rubbery to the touch. Cover and refrigerate, or cut into small squares equivalent to 1 tablespoon or more and freeze for use in preparing soups or stews.

IS STOCK NECESSARY?

It depends on the soup or stew. Some need stock for taste and body. *French Onion Soup*, 53, derives its rich colour and deep flavour from beef stock. Similarly, most single-vegetable soups need the depth of flavour that a savoury liquid brings. In some cases, stock is the very soul of the soup: *Matzo Ball Soup*, 33, is really chicken stock with matzo balls in it.

But when the main ingredients of a soup or stew are full of character, you may not want to mask their flavours by adding stock. The beetroot in *New York Deli Borscht*, 48, the vegetables in *Provençal Vegetable Soup*, 59, the meat in *Oxtail Soup*, 104, need nothing more than water to carry their powerful flavours. Likewise, most soups and stews based on beans and pulses, 65 to 72, do not require stock, their main ingredients being rich and earthy. Keep in mind that a few soups and stews can be prepared either with stock or without. *Minestrone*, 46, may have a warmer flavour with chicken stock, but it is also fine with water.

A classic stock – composed of many ingredients, simmered for hours, strained and reduced – is essential only for soups and stews where the broth is the main component. For most other recipes, an express broth, 28 to 29, will work perfectly well. So will a tinned stock. Low-sodium tinned stocks leave the cook freer to adjust the seasonings.

HOW TO STRAIN AND STORE STOCK

1 When the stock has finished cooking, strain it through a fine-mesh sieve (or a colander lined with a double layer of muslin or a coffee filter) into another pot or a large heatproof container and discard the solids.

2 Pressing heavily on the solids while straining may cloud the stock. We have recommended it for the vegetable stock recipes, where the extra flavour from the cooked vegetables is needed.

3 Do not let the stock sit out at room temperature for long as it is a good breeding ground for bacteria. Speed up the cooling process by placing the hot bowl, uncovered, in another bowl of iced water and stirring it a few times.

4 Once the stock cools enough so that it will not raise the temperature of your refrigerator, cover it tightly and chill it. When the stock is chilled, any fat will rise in a solid mass that must be removed before reheating. While cold, this fat layer (shown on chicken stock) actually protects the stock.

5 Stock will keep for 3 to 5 days in the refrigerator. If refrigerated for longer, after 3 days skim the solidified fat from the surface and boil the stock for 10 minutes, then refrigerate it for another 3 to 5 days.

6 For prolonged storage, transfer stock to litre or pint plastic containers or plastic freezer bags and freeze it. Small amounts of stock can also be frozen in ice cube trays. See also *Reducing Stock to a Glaze, opposite,* for other storage possibilities.

Vegetable Stock

About 1 litre (1½ pints)

Vegetable stocks allow for much improvision. Good additions include onions, carrots, potatoes, corncobs, fennel, fresh herbs, ginger, garlic, washed organic vegetable skins and even a few tablespoons of lentils. Vegetables to avoid include those in the cabbage family (except when used deliberately and with discretion), aubergine and most strong greens (with the exception of kale); too many carrots or parsnips will turn the stock overly sweet. When possible, tailor the ingredients to suit the recipe the stock will be used in. For example, a stock accented with ginger and garlic would be good in many Oriental recipes.

Combine in a stockpot:

1 medium onion, sliced

**1 leek, white part only, cleaned
    thoroughly and sliced**

1 carrot, peeled and sliced

1 small turnip, peeled and sliced

6 cloves garlic, peeled and smashed

1.5 litres (2½ pints) cold water

1 Bouquet Garni, 17

Simmer gently, partially covered, until the vegetables are completely softened, 45 to 60 minutes. Strain into a clean pot or heatproof plastic container, pressing down on the vegetables to extract the juices. Season with:

**Salt and ground black pepper
    to taste (optional)**

Let cool, uncovered, then refrigerate until ready to use.

Roast Vegetable Stock

About 1 litre (1½ pints)

Preheat the oven to 200°C (400°F) Gas 6. Lightly grease a roasting tin. Toss together in the prepared tin and roast, stirring occasionally, until well browned, about 1 hour:

**250g (8oz) mushrooms or
    mushroom stems, wiped clean**

1 onion, quartered

**2 carrots, peeled and cut into
    5cm (2in) pieces**

8 cloves garlic, peeled and smashed

**1 small turnip, peeled and cut into
    5cm (2in) pieces**

Remove the vegetables to a stockpot, then deglaze the hot roasting tin by adding:

250ml (8floz) cold water

Scrape up any browned bits, then add the liquid to the pot along with:

1.5 litres (2½ pints) cold water

**1 Bouquet Garni, 17, including a
    pinch of crushed chilli flakes**

Simmer gently, uncovered, until the vegetables are completely softened, 45 to 60 minutes. Strain into a clean pot or heatproof plastic container, pressing down on the vegetables to extract the juices. Season with:

Salt to taste

Let cool, uncovered, then refrigerate until ready to use.

Prawn Stock

About 750ml (1¼ pints)

For a clear stock, omit the tomato purée.
Heat in a stockpot over medium-high heat:

2 tbsp vegetable oil

Add and cook, stirring occasionally, until the shells are bright pink and aromatic, about 15 minutes:

155g (5oz) uncooked prawn shells, well rinsed and drained (from about 1kg/2lb prawns)
2 small onions, diced

2 small carrots, peeled and diced
2 celery stalks, diced
Stir in:
2 tbsp tomato purée (optional)
Add:
1.5 litres (2½ pints) cold water
1 bay leaf
1½ tsp lightly crushed black peppercorns
Splash of Pernod or ¼ tsp fennel seeds (optional)

Bring almost to a boil, reduce the heat and simmer gently, partially covered, for 20 minutes. Strain into a clean pot or heatproof plastic container, pressing down on the shells to extract all the liquid. Let cool, uncovered, then refrigerate until ready to use.

Fish Stock

About 1.5 litres (2½ pints)

If fish bones are unavailable, use inexpensive whole fish. For a mild-tasting, all-purpose fish stock, avoid oily fish.
Combine in a stockpot over medium heat:

1kg (2lb) fish heads and bones, or whole fish, scaled, gutted, gills and viscera removed, rinsed well and drained
1 small onion, sliced
1 large leek, white and tender green parts, cleaned thoroughly and sliced
½ fennel bulb, sliced (optional)

1-2 cloves garlic (optional)
250ml (8floz) dry white wine (optional)
1.5 litres (2½ pints) cold water (or just enough to cover)
1 *Bouquet Garni*, 17

Bring to a boil, reduce the heat and simmer gently. Cook, uncovered, skimming often, for 30 to 40 minutes. Strain into a clean pot or heatproof plastic container. Let cool, uncovered, then refrigerate until ready to use.

FISH FUMET

Prepare *Fish Stock, left*, first cooking the vegetables over medium-low heat in 30g (1oz) butter until they begin to soften, about 5 minutes. Add the fish heads and bones and cook, stirring once or twice, until they begin to turn opaque, 5 minutes more. Be sure not to let the vegetables or fish brown. Add the wine, cold water and bouquet garni and continue as directed.

BAY LEAVES AND PEPPERCORNS

From a graceful evergreen tree, bay leaves are long, narrow, pointed, dark and leathery. Their flavour is pungent and complex – something between eucalyptus, mint, lemon and freshly cut grass.

Pepper berries are the fruit of a leafy green vine that has spikes of white flowers; the flowers become clusters of green berries. These green peppercorns have a mild fresh flavour. Black peppercorns are green berries that are piled up and fermented for a few days, then dried in the sun, to become hard, wrinkled and dark brown to black. Their flavour is rich and spicy, especially if the berries are Malabar peppercorns. Used whole to flavour soups and stews, the flavour of peppercorns is discreet; tie the whole berries in a piece of muslin, then remove them before serving. When peppercorns are freshly crushed with a pestle and mortar, most of their oils are retained and the flavour is extremely pungent.

Chicken Stock

About 2 litres (3¼ pints)

Using the lesser amount of chicken suggested here will result in a lighter stock (opposite), which will reinforce the flavour in many dishes without adding a pronounced chicken taste; the greater amount will yield a richer one.
Combine in a stockpot over medium heat:
2-2.75kg (4-5½ lb) chicken parts (backs, necks, wings, legs or thighs), or 1 whole 2-2.75kg (4-5½ lb) roasting chicken, well rinsed
4 litres (6½ pints) cold water (or just enough to cover)

Bring to a boil, reduce the heat and simmer gently. Skim often until impurities no longer appear, about 30 minutes. Add:
1 onion, coarsely chopped
1 carrot, peeled and coarsely chopped
1 celery stalk, coarsely chopped
1 *Bouquet Garni*, 17
Simmer, uncovered, for 3 hours, adding water as needed to cover. Strain into a clean pot or heatproof plastic container. Let cool, uncovered, then refrigerate. Remove the fat when ready to use.

COOKING ONIONS

Cooking onions are the common medium to large yellow, red, and white onions that never fail us at the supermarket. Skin colour has less to do with the flavour of a cooking onion than its variety and where it was grown. Generally, yellow onions are richly flavoured but on the sharp side when raw. Most sweeten when carefully cooked. White onions are often pungent when raw, but there are mild varieties like White Sweet Spanish. Generally speaking, Spanish is understood to mean a very large, mild, yellow onion. Red onions are usually on the sweet side and can be cooked the same way but do not store as well as most yellow and white onions. Cooking onions of all kinds should be tightly closed and very firm, without soft spots or black, powdery patches of mould. To store dried onions, spread them out – do not heap – in a cool, dry place. Wrap cut onions tightly in cling film and place in the vegetable drawer of the refrigerator.

BROWN (OR ROAST) CHICKEN STOCK

This chicken stock has a richer flavour than "white" chicken stock. It can be used for hearty chicken soups and stews or in place of beef stock.
Preheat the oven to 220°C (425°F) Gas 7. Prepare *Chicken Stock, above,* first combining the chicken parts and vegetables, without the bouquet garni, in a heavy roasting tin and roasting, stirring occasionally, until well browned, about 1 hour. Remove the chicken and vegetables to a stockpot and deglaze the roasting tin by adding 250ml (8floz) water and scraping up any browned bits. Add the liquid to the pot along with water to cover, about 4 litres (6½ pints), and the bouquet garni. Continue as directed.

Turkey Stock

3 to 5 litres (5 to 8 pints)

This stock is the perfect use for a leftover Christmas turkey carcass and the accompanying bits of meat. If the carcass is very large, break it into pieces before adding it to the pot. Turkey stock can be substituted in any dish calling for chicken stock.
Barely cover with cold water in a large stockpot over medium heat:
1 turkey carcass, from a 6-15kg (12-25lb) turkey, broken up
Bring to a boil, reduce the heat, and simmer gently. Skim often until impurities no longer appear, about 30 minutes. Add:
1 onion, quartered
1 carrot, peeled and cut into 2.5cm (1in) pieces
1 celery stalk, cut into 2.5cm (1in) pieces
1 *Bouquet Garni*, 17
Simmer, uncovered, for 3 hours. Skim any impurities that rise and add water as needed to cover. Strain into a clean pot or heatproof plastic container. Let cool, uncovered, then refrigerate. Remove the fat when ready to use.

Brown Beef Stock

About 2.5 litres (4 pints)

The combination of beef and chicken bones produces a hearty stock in half the time it takes to make Classic Beef Stock, right.

Preheat the oven to 220°C (425°F) Gas 7. Lightly oil a roasting tin. Place in the prepared pan and roast for 15 minutes:

1.5kg (3lb) meaty beef shanks, cut into 5cm (2in) pieces, or oxtails, split into chunks, or a combination

Add:

500g (1lb) chicken parts (backs, necks, wings, legs or thighs), well rinsed

2 medium onions, quartered

2 carrots, peeled and thickly sliced

2 celery stalks, cut into 5cm (2in) pieces

Roast, stirring occasionally to prevent the vegetables from burning, until the bones are well browned, about 40 minutes. Transfer the meat and vegetables to a stockpot, carefully pour off any excess grease without discarding the caramelized cooking juices, and add to the hot roasting tin:

500ml (16floz) cold water

Scrape up any browned bits, then add the liquid to the pot along with:

3.5 litres (5½ pints) cold water (or just enough to cover)

Bring to a boil over medium heat, skim off the impurities, reduce the heat and simmer gently. Skim often until impurities no longer appear, about 30 minutes. Add:

1 leek, split lengthwise, cleaned, and cut into 5cm (2in) pieces

1 *Bouquet Garni*, 17, including 1 whole clove

Simmer, uncovered, for 4 hours, skimming as necessary and adding water as needed to cover. Strain into a clean pot or heatproof plastic container. Let cool, uncovered, then refrigerate. Remove the fat when ready to use.

CLASSIC BEEF STOCK

Prepare *Brown Beef Stock*, left, substituting 2.5kg (5lb) beef bones, preferably knucklebones, for the beef shins and chicken. Cut the vegetables into larger pieces and simmer the stock for 8 hours.

LAMB STOCK

About 1.75 litres (2¾ pints)

Lamb Stock (below) boosts the flavour of lamb soups and stews. Do not use it in recipes calling for fowl or other kinds of meat. Its flavour is assertive and can easily overpower more delicate foods. Prepare *Brown Beef Stock*, left, substituting 1kg (2lb) lamb shoulder chops, well trimmed, for the beef and chicken and decreasing the onions, carrots, celery and water by one-half. Omit the leek. Simmer for 3 hours.

Game Stock

About 2 litres (3¼ pints)

This stock can be made with rabbit or with duck, guinea hen or other small game birds.

Combine in a stockpot over medium heat:

One 1.5kg (3lb) rabbit or fowl, or 1.5kg (3lb) meaty game bones, rinsed and drained

4 litres (6½ pints) cold water

Bring to a boil, reduce the heat, and simmer gently. Skim often until impurities no longer appear, about 30 minutes.

Add:

1 medium onion, coarsely chopped

1 carrot, peeled and cut into 2.5cm (1in) pieces

1 celery stalk, cut into 2.5cm (1in) pieces

1 *Bouquet Garni*, 17

Simmer, uncovered, for 2½ hours, adding water as needed to cover. Strain into a clean pot or heatproof plastic container. Let cool, uncovered, then refrigerate. Remove the fat when ready to use.

White Veal Stock

About 2 litres (3¼ pints)

The comparatively mild flavour of this stock makes it highly versatile. Blanching the veal breast and bones by briefly boiling them and discarding the water helps create a clear stock. Ask your butcher to split the veal bones.

Cover with cold water in a stockpot over high heat:

750g (1½ lb) veal breast
750g (1½ lb) veal knucklebones, split

Bring to a boil. Immediately drain and rinse the veal, the bones and the pot. Return the veal breast and bones to the pot along with:

375g (12oz) chicken parts (backs, necks, wings, legs or thighs), well rinsed

3 litres (5 pints) cold water (or just enough to cover)

Bring to a boil, skim off the impurities and reduce the heat. Simmer gently for about 20 minutes. Add:

2 large onions, coarsely chopped
2 medium leeks, white and tender green parts, cleaned thoroughly and chopped
2 carrots, peeled and coarsely chopped
1 celery stalk, coarsely chopped
1 *Bouquet Garni*, 17

Simmer, uncovered, for 3 to 4 hours, adding water as needed to cover. Strain into a clean pot or heatproof plastic container. Let cool, uncovered, then refrigerate. Remove the fat when ready to use.

BROWN VEAL STOCK

Preheat the oven to 220°C (425°F) Gas 7. Lightly grease a roasting tin. Proceed as for *White Veal Stock*, left, but first roast the veal breast and bones in the prepared tin for 15 minutes; add the chicken and vegetables and roast until well browned, about 1 hour. Remove the meat and vegetables to a stockpot, carefully pour off any excess grease without discarding the caramelized cooking juices, and add 250ml (8floz) cold water or wine (red or white) to the hot roasting tin. Scrape up browned bits and add the liquid to the pot with cold water to cover. Bring to a boil, reduce the heat and simmer gently, skimming often for the first 30 minutes. Add the bouquet garni and continue as directed.

Dashi

About 1 litre (1½ pints)

One of the bases of traditional Japanese cuisine, this stock is made quickly, from just two ingredients – kombu, or kelp, and katsuobushi, or dried bonito flakes, also referred to as smoky fish flakes – both of which can be found in Oriental markets or health food shops. Dashi should be used within 4 to 5 days of preparation.

It should not be boiled or cooked for too long, and it does not freeze well. When reheating, do not boil.

Combine in a stockpot over high heat:

One 13 x 10cm (5 x 4in) piece kombu (kelp)

1.12 litres (1¾ pints) cold water

Bring almost to a boil. Immediately remove from the heat and stir in:

5 tbsp loosely packed *katsuobushi* (dried bonito flakes)

Let stand until the flakes begin to sink, 2 to 3 minutes (opposite). Remove the kombu with tongs. Strain the stock at once into a clean pot or heatproof plastic container. Let cool, uncovered, then refrigerate until ready to use.

Chicken-Enriched Dashi (Tori-Gara Dashi)

About 1 litre (1½ pints)

Cover with cold water in a stockpot over high heat:

500g (1lb) chicken parts (backs, necks, wings, legs or thighs), well rinsed

Bring to a boil. Immediately drain and rinse the chicken parts and the pot. Return the chicken to the pot along with:

One 13 x 10cm (5 x 4in) piece kombu (kelp)

1.5 litres (2½ pints) cold water

Bring to a boil, reduce the heat and simmer gently. Cook, uncovered, skimming often, for 20 to 25 minutes. Season with:

1 tbsp light or dark soy sauce

Remove from the heat and stir in:

5 tbsp loosely packed *katsuobushi* (dried bonito flakes)

Let stand until the flakes begin to sink, 2 to 3 minutes. Remove the kombu with tongs. Strain the stock into a clean pot or heatproof plastic container. Let cool, uncovered, then refrigerate until ready to use.

KELP AND BONITO FLAKES

Sold as "Dashi Kombu", an 185g (6oz) packet of kelp is enough to make six batches of broth for 4 to 6 people. The whitish coating on kelp is natural. Kelp should never be washed, or it will lose flavour. Kelp keeps indefinitely if stored tightly sealed.

Bonito flakes are dried, salted, fermented fish flakes. Bonito flakes will keep indefinitely on a cool, dark shelf in the pantry.

About Broths

Unlike stocks, which are made primarily from bones, broths are made from meat (except for vegetable broth), and they cook for shorter periods of time. The resulting liquid has a fresher, more definable flavour but less body than a stock. For this reason, broths are ideal for soups. Most of the ready-prepared stocks sold today are closer to broths and are best used in soups, not sauces, since they are often seasoned with salt and other seasonings, making it inadvisable to boil them down.

CHIPOTLE PEPPER

Chipotle peppers (dried smoked jalapeños) are making great gains in popularity for their intense, rich, smoky flavour. They show up everywhere, from tinned tomato sauce (adobo) to stews, soups, salsas, sauces and pickles. There are two types of chipotles, both made from different cultivars of the jalapeño. The first is the black-red chilli chipotle (also known as the chipotle colorado, mora or morita); this small chipotle (2.5-4cm/1-1½ in long and 1cm/½ in wide) is prized for its sweet, smoked flavour and its dark, rosewood colour. The second type, usually called chipotle meco, is larger (7.5-10cm/3-4in long by 2.5cm/1in wide) and pale brown in colour, with a more tobacco-like taste and usually less heat.

Express Fish Broth

About 1 litre (1 ½ pints)

When you haven't the time or inclination to procure fish bones for fish stock, the combination of bottled clam juice and tinned chicken broth or stock provides a decent substitute. If you have any fish trimmings on hand, throw them in as well.

Heat in a medium, heavy frying pan:

1½ tsp olive oil

Add:

1 carrot, peeled and finely chopped

1 small onion or large leek, finely chopped

1 clove garlic, finely chopped

Cook, stirring, over medium-high heat until soft. Add:

125ml (4floz) dry vermouth

Stir for about 1 minute, then blend in:

Four 250ml (8floz) bottles clam juice

375ml (12floz) mild chicken broth

Any fish trimmings on hand (optional)

¼ small lemon (optional)

Simmer for 20 minutes, skimming and stirring occasionally. Strain into a clean pot or heatproof plastic container. Let cool, uncovered, then refrigerate until ready to use.

Express Shellfish Chipotle Broth

About 625ml (1 pint)

This light but highly flavourful broth is good enough to be used as a sauce. Ladle a little over vegetables, pulses or seafood immediately before serving.

Combine in a large saucepan over medium heat:

75g (2½oz) uncooked prawn shells, well rinsed and drained (from about 500g/1lb prawns)

2 tsp tomato purée

½ tsp chopped chipotle peppers in adobo sauce, or to taste

Large pinch of saffron

125ml (4floz) dry white wine

Bring almost to a boil, reduce the heat, and simmer gently, partially covered, for 5 to 10 minutes. Add:

625ml (1 pint) *Chicken Stock*, 22

Simmer for 10 minutes more. Strain through a fine-mesh sieve and let the stock rest for a few minutes to allow any solids to settle. Carefully transfer to a clean saucepan or heat-proof plastic container, leaving the solids behind. Use immediately or let cool, uncovered, then refrigerate until ready to use.

Chicken Broth

About 3 litres (5 pints)

Once this broth is made, the chicken can be removed and used in soup or other dishes calling for cooked chicken.

Combine in a stockpot over medium heat:

1 whole 1.75-2kg (3½-4lb) chicken, well rinsed
3 litres (5 pints) cold water

Bring almost to a boil, reduce the heat and simmer gently, skimming often until impurities no longer appear. Meanwhile, pulse in a food processor until finely chopped:

1 medium onion, cut into eighths
1 carrot, peeled and cut into 5cm (2in) pieces
1 celery stalk, cut into 5cm (2in) pieces

Add the chopped vegetables to the pot. Simmer, uncovered, until the chicken is cooked, about 40 minutes. Remove the chicken and reserve. Strain the broth into a clean pot or heatproof plastic container. Let cool, uncovered, then refrigerate. Remove the fat when ready to use.

Express Chicken Broth

About 1 litre (1½ pints)

This broth can also be made with tinned beef broth or consommé; just omit the giblets.

Combine in a heavy saucepan:

1.25 litres (2 pints) ready-prepared reduced-sodium chicken broth
Any chicken giblets, trimmings or bones to hand (optional)
Contents of 1 *Bouquet Garni*, 17 (no need to wrap)

Cut into 2.5cm (1in) pieces and pulse in a food processor until finely chopped:

1 small onion
1 small carrot
1 small celery stalk, with leaves
1 leek, white part only, cleaned, or 3 whole spring onions
1 small clove garlic (optional)

Bring almost to a boil over medium-high heat, reduce the heat and simmer gently for about 30 minutes. Strain into a clean pot or heatproof plastic container. Let cool, uncovered, then refrigerate. Remove the fat when ready to use.

Express Beef Broth

About 1 litre (1½ pints)

This broth has a good, beefy flavour.

Combine in a stockpot over medium heat:

750g (1½ lb) boneless beef chuck, cut into 2.5cm (1in) cubes and pulsed in a food processor until coarsely chopped
1.25 litres (2 pints) cold water

Bring almost to a boil, reduce the heat and simmer gently, skimming often until impurities no longer appear. Add:

1 onion, cut into 2.5cm (1in) pieces
1 large leek, white and tender green parts, cleaned thoroughly and chopped
1 carrot, peeled and sliced
1 tbsp tomato purée
5 parsley stems
½ tsp dried thyme
3 black peppercorns, lightly crushed
1 whole clove

Simmer, uncovered, for 1 hour. Strain into a clean pot or heatproof plastic container. Let cool, uncovered, then refrigerate. Remove the fat when ready to use. The stock will separate, so whisk before using.

VEGETABLE BROTH

Use this method to extract the most flavour from the vegetables. Cooking the vegetables before adding them to the stockpot helps to express their flavour. This broth may not need to simmer as long as Vegetable Stock. Prepare Vegetable Stock, 20, first cooking the vegetables over medium heat in 30g (1oz) unsalted butter or oil, stirring occasionally, until they are wilted, about 15 minutes. Add the water and seasonings and continue as directed.

ABOUT
CLEAR STOCKS
WITH ADDITIONS

*T*his is one category of soups for which a tasty, full-bodied homemade stock is strongly recommended. You can intensify the flavour of a light stock by simmering it to evaporate some of the water. Or simmer it with chopped vegetables – finely diced carrots, celery and onions – and perhaps fresh herbs, then strain out the vegetables. The ultimate broth is consommé, 32, enriched with both meat and vegetables and clarified with egg whites.

Many of the recipes in this section call for chicken stock, because it is easy to prepare and seems to have the most universal appeal. Feel free to substitute any of the stocks provided in About Stocks & Broths, 13.

Chicken Noodle Soup, 33

Chicken or Beef Consommé

About 1.65 litres (2⅔ pints)

Clear, intensely flavourful consommé, one of the glories of classical French cooking, makes an elegant start to a formal dinner party. For a clear consommé, the stock must be completely free of grease. For particularly strong consommé, simmer 4 litres (6½ pints) of degreased stock until reduced by half before clarifying it.

Combine in a food processor:

1 small onion, quartered

1 small carrot, peeled and cut into 5cm (2in) pieces

1 small celery stalk, cut into 5cm (2in) pieces

2 tbsp fresh parsley leaves

½ tsp fresh thyme leaves

Pulse until coarsely chopped. Add:

500g (1lb) boneless, skinless chicken breasts, fat trimmed, cut into 5cm (2in) pieces, or 750g (1½ lb) beef round or rump steak, fat trimmed, cut into 5cm (1in) pieces

Pulse until chopped but not puréed.

Remove to a medium bowl. Add:

3 large egg whites

Stir together well. Warm in a soup pot, over low heat:

2 litres (3¼ pints) Chicken Stock, 22, Classic Beef Stock, 24 or Brown Beef Stock, 24, thoroughly degreased

Whisk in the vegetable mixture. Very slowly bring to a simmer without boiling, occasionally stirring and scraping the bottom of the pot to prevent burning until the egg foam rises to the surface, about 30 minutes. (Be careful not to stir after the broth reaches a simmer.) When the egg foam starts to solidify, make a small hole in the centre with the end of a wooden spoon. Continue to simmer very gently until the egg foam mixture is solid, about 30 minutes more. Remove the pot from the heat. Line a sieve with a slightly dampened muslin or tea towel. Gently move the foam to the side of the pot and ladle out the consommé. Strain the consommé through the sieve into a large saucepan. Season with:

1 tsp salt, or to taste

Heat through, then ladle into warmed bowls.

CONSOMMÉ BRUNOISE

In classical French cooking, a brunoise is a mixture of finely diced vegetables. This recipe uses three vegetables most basic to the French kitchen. Prepare Chicken or Beef Consommé, above, adding with the salt: 2 tbsp very finely diced leeks (white part only), 2 tbsp very finely diced carrots, and 2 tbsp very finely diced celery. Simmer gently until the vegetables are tender, about 5 minutes. Ladle into warmed bowls.

Chicken Noodle Soup

About 1 litre (1½ pints)

Using homemade stock in this recipe makes all the difference, transforming a dependable standard into a great soup. If you do make your own stock, remove some of the chicken meat from the bones when the stock is done and return it to the soup. For variety, try stirring in a peeled, seeded and diced tomato and a teaspoon of chopped fresh herbs, such as tarragon, parsley, dill or basil, just before serving the soup.

Bring to a boil in a medium saucepan:

1 litre (1½ pints) Chicken Stock, 22, or Brown Chicken Stock, 22

Stir in:

90g (3oz) fine egg noodles or 60g (2oz) thin fresh or dried pasta

Cook until the pasta is tender but firm, 4 to 5 minutes. Season with:

2 tbsp chopped fresh parsley

Salt to taste

Pinch of ground black pepper

Ladle into warmed bowls.

Chicken Rice or Barley Soup

About 1 litre (1½ pints)

With simple additions, flavourful homemade chicken stock can be transformed into a multitude of other soups. (Vegetarians can substitute Vegetable Stock, 20.) If you are adding grains and vegetables, add the vegetables when the grains are almost cooked.

Bring to a simmer in a medium saucepan:

1 litre (1½ pints) Chicken Stock, 22, or Brown Chicken Stock, 22

½ tsp salt

Stir in:

3 tbsp long-grain rice or 2 tbsp pearl barley

Simmer until tender, about 15 minutes for rice, 30 to 45 minutes for barley.

Chicken Soup with Ravioli or Tortellini

Prepare Chicken Rice or Barley Soup, left, substituting ravioli or tortellini (quantity to taste) for the rice or barley. Simmer until tender but firm, 5 to 10 minutes. Any of the following can be added to or substituted for the additions above:

Stir in 5 minutes before the soup is fully cooked:

280g (9oz) sliced mixed vegetables, such as carrots, celery, tomatoes, and/or onions

Stir in 1 to 2 minutes before the soup is fully cooked:

125g (4oz) thinly sliced greens (escarole, kale or spinach), trimmed, washed and dried

Stir in any of the following just before serving:

1 tbsp dry sherry

Chopped basil or parsley

Pinch of ground black pepper

Matzo Ball Soup

About 1.5 litres (2½ pints); 12 to 14 large balls

This simple classic is wonderful with or without the optional additions.

Beat on medium speed for 1 minute:

4 large eggs

1 tsp salt

If desired, stir in:

90g (3oz) finely diced fennel; 2 tbsp snipped fresh dill and 4 tsp snipped fresh or dried chives; or 2 tbsp chopped fresh parsley and 2 tbsp snipped fresh dill (optional)

Stir in:

90ml (3floz) soda water

Fold in until well blended:

90g (3oz) matzo meal

¼ tsp ground black pepper

1 tsp curry powder (optional)

1-2 tsp finely chopped peeled fresh ginger, or 1 tsp ground (optional)

Cover and refrigerate for 1 to 4 hours. With wet hands, form the matzo balls. Drop the balls into a large pot of boiling salted water, cover, reduce the heat and simmer for 20 minutes. When the matzo balls are almost finished, heat in a soup pot:

1.5 litres (2½ pints) Chicken Stock, 22

Season with:

1¼ tsp salt

¼ tsp ground black pepper (optional)

When the matzo balls are finished, add them to the stock. Ladle the stock into warmed bowls and add 2 matzo balls to each serving.

Chinese Egg Drop Soup

About 1 litre (1½ pints)

A simple, delicate soup.
Combine in a large saucepan and simmer, partially covered, for 15 minutes:

1 litre (1½ pints) Chicken Stock, 22
2 large slices fresh ginger
2 large cloves garlic, smashed
and peeled

Discard the ginger and garlic. Stir together in a small bowl:

1 tbsp cornflour
3 tbsp water

Bring the soup to a low simmer and add the cornflour mixture. Stir until the soup is slightly thickened. Stir in:

1 tsp salt
⅛ tsp ground black pepper

Whisk together thoroughly in a small bowl:

1 large egg
1 tsp vegetable oil

Bring the soup to a very low simmer and pour the egg mixture in a large circle on the surface of the soup. Once the egg sets, stir gently. Stir in:

2 spring onions, diagonally sliced
2 tbsp chopped fresh coriander

Ladle into warmed bowls.

Italian Parmesan and Egg Soup (Stracciatella)

About 750ml (24floz)

A Roman speciality, stracciatella derives its name from the word straccetti, little rags – describing the strands of cooked egg that float in the broth.

Bring to a simmer in a medium saucepan:

750ml (24floz) Chicken Stock, 22

Meanwhile, whisk together in a small bowl until well blended:

1 large egg
1½ tbsp grated Parmesan cheese
1 tbsp dry breadcrumbs
2 tbsp chopped fresh parsley
1 small clove garlic, finely chopped

Stir this mixture rapidly into the simmering stock and stir until the egg is set, 30 to 60 seconds.
Garnish with:

Freshly grated or ground nutmeg or grated lemon zest

Ladle into warmed bowls.

Greek Lemon Soup

About 1 litre (1½ pints)

Unlike stracciatella, where the eggs are supposed to separate, here the eggs are blended to create a smooth, creamy texture. This is done by adding a little of the hot stock to the eggs before they are added to the soup to prevent them from curdling.

Bring to a rolling boil in a medium saucepan:

750ml (24floz) Chicken Stock, 22
100g (3½ oz) long-grain rice

Reduce the heat, cover and simmer until the rice is tender, about 20 minutes. In a medium bowl, whisk just enough to combine and be uniform in colour:

2 large eggs
60ml (2floz) fresh lemon juice

Stir 2 tablespoons of the hot stock into the egg mixture. To prevent curdling, gradually pour the egg mixture into the hot,

not boiling, soup while stirring constantly.
Season with:

1-2 tbsp fresh lemon juice (optional)
Salt and ground black pepper to taste

Ladle into warmed bowls.
Garnish with:

Chopped fresh parsley or snipped fresh dill

Miso and Miso Soups

Miso, a fermented paste made from soybeans, comes in a variety of colours (from white to yellow to red) and textures (smooth or chunky), depending on the length of fermentation and the addition of grains such as barley or rice. As a general rule, the darker the miso, the longer it has been fermented and the stronger and saltier it will taste. Lighter miso, fermented for a shorter period, is sweeter. Barley miso is earthy and well aged. Although miso rarely spoils, it loses its flavour after a few months. Keep opened containers in the refrigerator.

Miso soups are an essential part of the traditional Japanese breakfast, though soups thickened with miso also appear at lunch and dinner. In Japan, there are many varieties of miso. Here are two basic miso soups, one based on the light-coloured, mellow miso that is popular in Kyoto and Osaka, and the other a dark-coloured, pungent red miso that is favoured in the Tokyo region.

Dark-Coloured Miso Soup with Sautéed Vegetables

Just over 1 litre (1½ pints)

This is a rich and flavourful miso soup.
Soak in cold water for 10 minutes:
1½ tsp dried *wakame* bits (optional)
Drain, squeeze out the excess liquid and divide the *wakame* among 4 soup bowls. Heat in a medium saucepan over high heat:
1 tsp vegetable oil
Add and cook, stirring, until slightly browned, about 1 minute:
2-3 fresh shiitake mushroom caps, thinly sliced
1 small leek (white part only), cleaned thoroughly and thinly sliced on a diagonal
Add:
Pinch of salt
½ tsp sake (optional)
Cook, stirring, until the leeks are wilted, about another minute. Stir in:
1 litre (1½ pints) *Dashi*, 27
1 tsp light or dark soy sauce
Cook over medium-low heat until warm. Place in a small bowl:
3-3½ tbsp red miso
Add about 60ml (2floz) of the warm dashi and whisk to dissolve the miso; then whisk this mixture back into the soup. Ladle the hot miso-thickened broth and vegetables over the *wakame*. Serve immediately.

WAKAME

Wakame is an edible seaweed. After the leaves of the plant have been soaked, they are briefly cooked in soups or can be used to make a salad. *Wakame* makes a nice addition to miso soups. *Wakame* is sold dried and packaged, sometimes labelled *ito-wakame*. To reconstitute dried *wakame*, simply soak it in tepid water for 20 minutes, to maintain its flavour and the seaweed's high nutritional value. If the stem of the seaweed is present, it should be discarded.

Light-Coloured Miso Soup with Simmered Vegetables

Just over 1 litre (1½ pints)

Autumn brings enormous (30cm/12in long) pure white, carrot-shaped, juicy radishes called mooli *or, in Japan,* daikon. *These radishes are mild in flavour and often added to soups.*

Bring to a simmer in a medium saucepan:
1 litre (1½ pints) *Dashi*, 27
Season with:
1 tsp light or dark soy sauce
Splash of sake (optional)

Stir in and simmer until barely tender, 2 to 3 minutes:
1 small carrot, peeled, halved lengthwise and thinly sliced
5cm (2in) piece mooli radish, peeled, halved lengthwise, and thinly sliced
Place in a small bowl:
3 tbsp light-coloured miso, such as shiro mugi miso (barley-enriched miso)

Add about 60ml (2floz) of the warm dashi and whisk to dissolve the miso; then whisk this mixture back into the soup. Divide among 4 bowls:
1 small spring onion, chopped
60g (2oz) firm tofu, cut into small cubes
Ladle the hot miso-thickened broth and vegetables into the bowls. Serve immediately.

Mongolian Hot Pot

About 2 litres (3¼ pints); 6 to 8 servings

A hot pot is a round basin with a sort of chimney in the middle containing smouldering coals to heat stock, shown below. This device can be found in Oriental shops or speciality cookware shops, but a fondue pot or electric frying pan, while not as dramatic, can easily be substituted. In China, diners cook their own meat and vegetables in the sizzlingly hot stock, then dip them into a sauce they assemble from a selection of seasonings set out on the table. When all the meat and vegetables have been eaten, the guests sip the remaining soup. This is a wonderful party dish. The meat is easier to slice thinly if frozen for 20 minutes first.

For the dipping sauce, purée in a blender:

125ml (4floz) rice vinegar
5 tbsp sugar or 4 tbsp honey

125ml (4floz) soy sauce
80ml (3floz) red miso or rinsed fermented black beans
60ml (2floz) toasted sesame oil
1 tbsp chopped peeled fresh ginger
2 tsp chilli oil, or more to taste
3 cloves garlic, finely chopped

Pour the sauce into individual serving bowls and garnish with:

Chopped spring onions (about 3 spring onions)
Chopped fresh coriander
Snipped fresh chives

Arrange decoratively on a platter:

1kg (2lb) beef sirloin steak or lamb loin, fat trimmed, thinly sliced
185g (6oz) sliced Chinese leaf
250g (8oz) firm tofu, cut into 16 pieces
250g (8oz) spinach, trimmed, washed and dried

To serve, bring the sauce and platter to the table. Bring to a boil:

2-2.5 litres (3¼-4 pints) Brown Beef Stock, 24

Pour the hot stock into a hot pot, fondue pot or electric frying pan at the table and keep at a simmer. With chopsticks or forks, diners hold the meat or vegetables in the simmering stock until done, then dip it into the sauce and eat. When the ingredients on the platter are finished, combine and let stand for 10 minutes:

125g (4oz) rice stick noodles, broken into small pieces
1.5 litres (2½ pints) hot water

Drain and add the noodles to the stock. Ladle the stock and noodles into each bowl over the remaining sauce.

ABOUT **VEGETABLE** SOUPS & STEWS

If you live near an open or farmers' market and have the time, shop there for the best seasonal produce from your area. As a general seasonal guide, prepare soups and stews using root vegetables and hearty vegetables, such as winter squash, during the cold months; soups and stews using more perishable produce, such as tomatoes and sweetcorn, are best cooked during the warm months.

Cut vegetables are often an integral part of a mixed-vegetable soup or stew. Cut them uniformly, to help ensure even cooking. When improvising a soup or stew using cut vegetables, bear in mind that some vegetables take longer than others to cook. Long-cooking vegetables, such as potatoes, should be added first, followed by vegetables such as carrots and green beans, leaving quick-cooking greens, such as spinach and chard, for last. To retain the colour in green vegetables, be careful not to cover or overcook the soup. Puréed green-vegetable soups should not cook long, or they will turn grey.

Old-Fashioned Vegetable Soup, 43

Butternut Squash Soup

About 2.25 litres (3⅔ pints)

Almost any winter squash can be used. For an unusual garnish, rinse and dry the squash seeds, toss them in 1½ tsp oil to lightly coat and bake them along with the squash until browned, then sprinkle them on the soup just before serving.

Preheat the oven to 200°C (400°F) Gas 6.

Place cut side down on an oiled baking tray:

1 medium to large butternut squash (about 1.75kg/3½ lb), halved and seeded

Bake until the squash can easily be pierced with a fork, about 1 hour. Let cool, then scoop the pulp from the squash skin and discard the skin. Melt or heat in a soup pot, over medium-low heat:

45g (1½ oz) unsalted butter or 3 tbsp vegetable oil

Add and cook, stirring, until tender but not browned, 5 to 10 minutes:

2 large leeks (white part only), cleaned thoroughly and chopped
4 tsp chopped peeled fresh ginger

Stir in the squash along with:

1 litre (1½ pints) Chicken Stock, 22, or any vegetable stock, 20

Bring to a simmer and cook, stirring and breaking up the squash with a spoon, for 20 minutes. Purée until smooth. Return to the pot and stir in:

500ml (16floz) chicken or vegetable stock

1½ tsp salt

Heat through. Ladle into warmed bowls. Garnish with:

Chopped fresh parsley or coriander
Croutons, 124
Toasted squash seeds (optional)

BUTTERNUT SQUASH

Butternut squash is beige and long necked with a bulb at one end. Inside the squash, the orange flesh is rich, sweet, dry and superb. These 2-3kg (4-6lb) squash have the least waste of any winter squash, since the neck is solid and just the bulb contains seeds.

Cream of Cauliflower Soup

About 1.5 litres (2½ pints)

This recipe is a blueprint for a multitude of vegetable soups, all delicious. To retain the colour in green vegetables, such as broccoli, do not cover or overcook the soup.

Heat in a soup pot over medium-low heat until the butter is melted:

60ml (2floz) water or stock

15g (½ oz) unsalted butter (optional)

Add and cook, covered, stirring occasionally, until tender but not browned, 5 to 10 minutes:

1 medium onion, coarsely chopped

2 cloves garlic, sliced

⅛ tsp ground nutmeg (optional)

Stir in:

Just over 1 litre (1½ pints) Chicken Stock, 22, or vegetable stock, 20

125ml (4floz) white wine (optional)

750g (1½ lb) trimmed cauliflower, coarsely chopped

Bring to a boil, reduce the heat and simmer until the cauliflower is tender, 15 to 20 minutes. Purée until smooth. Return to the pot and stir in:

60-125ml (2-4floz) single or double cream or milk

½ -1 tsp salt

⅛ tsp ground white or black pepper

Simmer briefly and ladle into warmed bowls. Garnish with:

Chopped fresh parsley or snipped fresh dill or chives

Serve with:

Croutons, 124

Old-Fashioned Vegetable Soup

About 1 litre (1½ pints)

Feel free to vary the vegetables in this soup. For the 750ml (24floz) of stock in the recipe, use 250g (8oz) diced vegetables. You could feature the finest vegetables from any one season, changing this soup all the year round. Remember that vegetables cook at varying rates. Start with the heartiest and finish with the most tender.

Bring to a boil over high heat, in a soup pot:

750ml (24floz) Classic Beef Stock, 24, Brown Beef Stock, 24, Chicken Stock, 22, or Vegetable Stock, 20

4 tbsp diced onions

4 tbsp diced carrots

4 tbsp sliced celery

4 tbsp diced potatoes

4 tbsp 2.5cm (1in) pieces green beans

4 tbsp sweetcorn kernels

4 tbsp petit pois peas

4 tbsp cooked borlotti beans

4 tbsp chopped green cabbage (optional)

1 clove garlic, finely chopped

1½ tsp tomato purée or 90g (3oz) chopped drained tinned or stewed tomatoes

Reduce the heat to low and simmer for 10 minutes. Stir in:

2 tbsp chopped fresh parsley

Salt and ground black pepper to taste

Ladle into warmed bowls and serve.

CREAM OF ASPARAGUS SOUP

Follow the recipe for *Cream of Cauliflower Soup, left*, omitting the nutmeg and using 1 litre (1½ pints) chicken stock and 125ml (4floz) dry vermouth or white wine (optional). Trim 750g (1½ lb) asparagus, discarding the tough ends and reserving the tips. Chop the stalks and add to the stock. Simmer for 5 minutes. Purée the soup, adding 60-125ml (2-4floz) double or single cream, salt to taste, ⅛ tsp black pepper and the reserved asparagus tips. Simmer for 3 to 5 minutes and serve.

CREAM OF BROCCOLI SOUP

Follow the recipe for *Cream of Cauliflower Soup, above left*, substituting broccoli for the cauliflower. Simmer the broccoli until tender but still brightly coloured, 5 to 8 minutes. Proceed with the basic recipe, using ground black, not white, pepper.

CREAM OF CARROT SOUP

Follow the recipe for *Cream of Cauliflower Soup, above left*, substituting carrots for the cauliflower, 1 tbsp chopped peeled fresh ginger for the garlic, and ½ tsp curry powder for the nutmeg; using 1 litre (1½ pints) stock and 250ml (8floz) fresh orange juice; and omitting the wine. Simmer for 15 minutes. Purée the soup, adding 60-125ml (2-4floz) double or single cream, salt to taste and ⅛ tsp ground black pepper. Simmer briefly and serve.

Mushroom Barley Soup

About 1 litre (1½ pints)

Combine and let stand until the mushrooms are softened, about 20 minutes:

7g (¼ oz) dried mushrooms, such as porcini or shiitake (about 3)
250ml (8floz) hot water

Remove the mushrooms and squeeze dry with paper towels. Reserve the soaking liquid. Dice the mushrooms finely and reserve. Heat in a soup pot over medium-low heat until the butter is melted:

15g (½ oz) unsalted butter
1 tbsp vegetable oil

Add and cook, stirring, until tender but not browned, 5 to 10 minutes:

155g (5oz) mushrooms, wiped clean and tough stems removed, coarsely chopped
1 small leek (white part only), cleaned thoroughly and diced
1 small onion, diced
1 medium celery stalk, diced
1 small carrot, diced
2 cloves garlic, finely chopped

Increase the heat slightly and add:

5 tbsp pearl barley

Cook, stirring, until lightly toasted, about 5 minutes. Stir in the reserved diced mushrooms. Strain the soaking liquid through a fine-mesh sieve lined with a dampened paper towel and stir it into the vegetable mixture along with:

1 litre (1½ pints) *Brown Beef Stock*, 24, or *Roast Vegetable Stock*, 20

Bring to a boil, reduce the heat and simmer, partially covered, until the barley is tender, about 40 minutes. Season with:

1 tbsp snipped fresh dill
½ tsp salt
½ tsp ground black pepper

Ladle into warmed bowls (opposite) and serve immediately.

Spring Onion and Mushroom Soup

About 1.75 litres (2¾ pints)

This soup uses the whole spring onion with stunning results. Select spring onions with the crispest leaves with no yellowing or tears, and shiny, bright, stalks. Use your favourite variety of mushroom or a combination of types.

Beat with a wooden spoon until light and fluffy:

60g (2oz) unsalted butter, softened

Add and stir together well:

5 bunches spring onions, very finely chopped

Remove to a soup pot and season with:

1 tsp salt
½ tsp ground white pepper

Cook, covered, over low heat for about 10 minutes. Do not brown the spring onions. Remove the pot from the heat. Stir in:

2 tbsp plain flour

Cook for 1 minute. Whisk in:

1 litre (1½ pints) *Chicken Stock*, 22

Bring to a boil, whisking, over medium heat. Reduce the heat and simmer for 10 minutes. Meanwhile, wipe clean, remove the tough ends of the stems only, and very thinly slice:

375g (12oz) mushrooms with stems

Remove the soup from the heat and stir in two-thirds of the mushrooms. Immediately push through a sieve or food mill. Stir in:

60-125ml (2-4floz) single cream

Gently heat the soup until hot, then stir in the remaining mushrooms. Ladle into warmed bowls. Top each serving with:

Sprinkle of cayenne pepper
Dollop of sour cream

PREPARING MUSHROOMS

Clean mushrooms with a soft brush or wipe with a damp cloth. If the mushrooms are very grimy, rinse quickly under cold running water and pat dry. Never soak mushrooms – their delicate tissues will absorb water. If desired, slice 3mm (⅛ in) off the bottom of the stems to refresh them but do not discard the flavourful stems. If only caps are called for in a recipe, cut the stem flush with the cap. Either chop the stems fairly fine, toss them until lightly browned in a little butter, and add them to the dish or use within a day to flavour something else. Use intense heat when cooking mushrooms, and cook just enough to lightly brown and heat them through.

Minestrone

About 2.5 litres (4 pints)

Minestrone embraces a legion of hearty vegetable and bean soups from Italy. This one is a melding of styles and is equally good served hot or warm. It uses pancetta, the Italian version of bacon from the pork belly (pancia). If substituting bacon for pancetta, use unsmoked rather than smoked.

Heat over medium heat in a large soup pot, until the pancetta or bacon has released its fat, 2 to 3 minutes:

2 tbsp extra-virgin olive oil

30g (1oz) pancetta or 2 slices bacon, chopped (optional)

Add and cook, stirring, until the greens are beginning to wilt, 5 to 10 minutes:

1 medium onion, chopped

1 large carrot, peeled and chopped

2 medium celery stalks with leaves, chopped

10cm (4in) sprig fresh rosemary, or 1 tsp dried

4 tbsp fresh basil leaves, chopped

4 tbsp fresh parsley leaves, chopped

2 cloves garlic, finely chopped

½ small head green cabbage, chopped

3 Swiss chard leaves, washed, dried, and chopped

Cover, and cook until the vegetables are tender, about 10 minutes. Stir in:

400g (14oz) tin whole tomatoes, drained and broken into pieces

Cook, stirring, over medium-high heat for 3 to 5 minutes. Stir in:

500g (16oz) tinned *borlotti* or pinto beans, rinsed and drained, half of them mashed

2.5 litres (4 pints) *Chicken Stock*, 22, or water

2 tsp salt

Bring to a boil, reduce heat and simmer, partially covered, 30 minutes. Remove the rosemary sprig. Stir in:

125g (4oz) orzo pasta

Continue to simmer for 15 minutes. Ladle into warmed bowls and drizzle over each serving:

Extra-virgin olive oil

Sprinkle with:

Ground black pepper to taste

Smooth Potato Leek Soup (Potage Parmentier)

About 2 litres (3¼ pints)

Potatoes and leeks make magic together. This divine synergy is reflected in two soups. The one here is a simple stock- or water-based soup. Vichyssoise, *right, is a smooth, cream-enriched version. Thin the Smooth Potato Leek Soup, if necessary, with a bit more water or stock. For extra smoothness, push through a sieve after it has been puréed in a food processor.*

Melt in a soup pot, over low heat:

45g (1½ oz) unsalted butter, or 15g (½ oz) butter and 60ml (2floz) water

Add and cook, stirring, until tender but not browned, about 20 minutes:

8 large leeks (white part only), cleaned thoroughly and chopped

Stir in:

3 medium or 2 large baking potatoes, peeled and thinly sliced

1.25 litres (2 pints) Chicken Stock, 22, Vegetable Stock, 20, or water

Bring to a boil, reduce the heat and simmer until the potatoes are soft, about 30 minutes. Purée until smooth. Season with:

Salt to taste

¼ tsp ground white or black pepper

Thin, if necessary, with additional:

Stock or water

Reheat gently, then ladle into warmed bowls.

VICHYSSOISE

The "classic French" soup was invented by French chef Louis Diat around 1910. During the Second World War, when the French spa town of Vichy became the capital of the collaborationist government, this soup was served under a variety of names.

Prepare Smooth Potato Leek Soup, *left, adding 125-250ml (4-8floz) double cream, or a combination of milk and cream. Season with salt and ground black pepper to taste and thin if necessary. Garnish with snipped fresh chives, if desired. Serve hot or cold.*

PREPARING LEEKS

To julienne or slice leeks, trim off the root and the dark green leaves; if the pale green part is tender, leave about 2.5cm (1in) attached to the white part. For julienne, cut the leek lengthwise in half, then cut the halves into 5cm (2in) lengths and slice lengthwise. For slices, cut the halves crosswise into half slices.

The layers of a leek can contain dirt, since the white stalks are "blanched", buried in earth to keep them pale, so washing them thoroughly and properly is important. Swish chopped, julienned, or sliced leeks in a large bowl of cool water. Let them stand a few minutes while the dirt falls to the bottom (**1**).

Lift them out with a sieve. Repeat if there is a lot of dirt left in the bowl (**2**).

If you are using leeks that are simply halved lengthwise, soak them in water for 15 minutes to loosen the dirt, gently swish them around, and rinse under cool water, fanning the leaves open as you rinse if they are especially dirty.

Slender leeks are especially nice sliced into salads, barbecued and served hot, or steamed and served at room temperature. Thicker leeks are wonderful braised or in soups and stews. Be careful not to overcook leeks, as the layers are very thin.

Cabbage Soup

About 2 litres (3¼ pints)

We sampled this soup in a Paris bistro, where we discovered that a garnish of Roquefort adds just the right finish. Serve thick slices of baguette that have been toasted alongside – the toasted bread is good for dunking and for soaking up the soup.

Heat in a soup pot over medium-low heat:

2 tbsp olive or other vegetable oil

Add and cook, stirring, until tender but not browned, 5 to 10 minutes:

2 small leeks (white part only), cleaned thoroughly and chopped

2 medium onions, diced

2 tbsp chopped garlic

Stir in:

1 litre (1½ pints) *Chicken Stock, 22*

500ml (16floz) water

2 large carrots, sliced

**¾ tsp caraway seeds, or
    1 tsp if garnishing
    with Roquefort cheese**

Bring to a boil and stir in:

2 small potatoes, peeled and diced

Reduce the heat and simmer until the potatoes are cooked, about 15 minutes. Stir in:

375g (12oz) shredded green cabbage

Continue to simmer until the cabbage is wilted, about 15 minutes, adding a little water to cover, if necessary. Stir in:

1 tsp salt

¼ tsp ground black pepper, or to taste

4 tbsp chopped fresh parsley

Ladle into warmed bowls. Sprinkle each serving with:

1 tbsp crumbled Roquefort or other blue cheese (optional)

New York Deli Borscht

About 1.25 litres (2 pints)

About the only thing deli borscht has in common with traditional Russian Borscht, 97, is the presence of beetroot. This version is light and contains no fat. It is usually served cold but is also satisfying hot. For a more substantial dish, add warm, quartered new potatoes. Though many types of beetroots are available these days, use a red beetroot for this soup. If you find unwilted greens attached to your beetroots, wash and dry them, then chop and stir them in at the last minute for a nontraditional touch. This borscht can be puréed if a smooth soup is desired.

Combine in a soup pot:

750ml (24floz) water

**500g (1lb) beetroot, peeled and
    cut into thin strips**

**1 large carrot, peeled and cut into
    thin strips (optional)**

1 clove garlic, finely chopped

Bring to a boil, reduce the heat and simmer until the beetroots are tender, 5 to 10 minutes. Stir in:

2 tbsp fresh lemon juice

1½ tsp salt

⅛ tsp ground black pepper

Serve hot or cold, garnished with:

Sour cream

Snipped fresh dill

PREPARING BEETROOT

A source of sugar, beetroot is an intensely sweet vegetable with a trace of sharpness. Once there was just the crimson beetroot, but now beetroot is also gold, orange, white and striped. Beetroot is best from summer until early winter. When selecting a bunch of beetroot, choose the bunch with the smallest leaves that are in the best condition. The greens are an indication of freshness for the roots; if they look moist and fresh, the roots will be too.

Cut off the leaves, leaving 2.5-5cm (1-2in) stem on the beetroot, and keep the rootlets, or tails, in place (**1**).

Pack the beetroot and leaves separately in perforated plastic vegetable bags and store in the refrigerator drawer. Scrub beetroot well before cooking (**2**).

Fresh Tomato Soup

About .l litre (1½ pints)

A simple, clean-tasting soup (opposite).
Heat in a soup pot, over medium-low heat:

2 tbsp olive oil, preferably extra virgin

Add and cook, stirring, until tender but not browned, 5 to 10 minutes:

1 medium onion, coarsely chopped

Stir in:

1.5kg (3lb) ripe tomatoes, peeled, seeded and chopped, with juices

Simmer until the tomatoes are covered in their own liquid, about 25 minutes. Purée until smooth. Return to the pot and stir in:

¾ tsp salt

¼ tsp ground black pepper

Serve hot or cold.

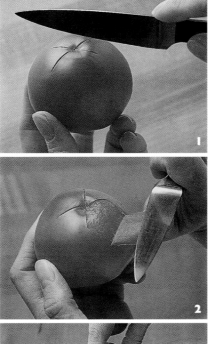

CREAM OF TOMATO SOUP

Prepare *Fresh Tomato Soup, above.* Stir in 60ml (2floz) double cream. Gently heat through. Serve immediately.

PEELING AND SEEDING TOMATOES

Cut a small X in the bottom – do not cut the flesh (**1**). Ease the tomatoes one by one into a pot of boiling water. Leave ripe tomatoes in for about 15 seconds, barely ripe tomatoes in for twice as long. Lift them out with a sieve and drop into a bowl of iced water to stop the cooking. Pull off the skin with the knife (**2**). If the skin sticks, return the tomato to the boiling water for another 10 seconds and repeat. If the dish can do with a touch of smoky flavour, hold the tomato on a long-handled fork over the burner, turning it until the skin splits. Do not plunge in water, but peel as above.

Cut it crosswise in half (between the top and bottom). Squeeze each half gently over a sieve set in a bowl to catch the juice, which you can add to soup. Run the tip of a finger into each of the cavities and flick out the mass of seeds (**3**).

Mushroom Soup

About 1.5 litres (2½ pints)

Slice rather than chop the mushrooms for a meaty texture and a handsome look.
Heat in a soup pot over high heat until the butter is melted:

3½ tbsp extra-virgin olive oil

15g (½ oz) unsalted butter or additional 1 tbsp olive oil

Add:

750g (1½ lb) mushrooms (at least 375g/12oz wild), wiped clean and tough stems removed, sliced

90g (3oz) chopped shallots

Cook, stirring often, until the mushrooms are wilted, about 5 minutes. Add:

3 tbsp dry sherry or Madeira

5 tbsp plain flour

1 tsp dried thyme, or 1 tbsp chopped fresh thyme

Reduce heat to low and cook, stirring constantly and scraping the bottom of the pan, for 5 minutes. Stir in:

Just over 1 litre (1½ pints) Brown Chicken Stock, 22, or any vegetable stock, 20

½ to 1 tsp salt

¾ tsp ground black pepper

Bring to a boil, reduce the heat to medium and simmer until slightly thickened, about 20 minutes. Ladle into warmed bowls. Garnish with:

Chopped fresh parsley or fresh thyme leaves

Tuscan Bread and Tomato Soup (Pappa al Pomodoro)

About 1 litre (1½ pints)

Make this favourite country soup from Tuscany with fresh tomatoes in high summer and eat it at room temperature, or prepare it with tinned tomatoes in winter and serve hot. To stay true to the goodness of the soup, use a bread made without sugar.

Preheat the oven to 95°C (200°F) Gas ¼.

Dry in the oven for 15 to 20 minutes:

2 or 3 thick slices country bread

Alternatively, use stale bread. Heat in a soup pot, over medium heat:

3 tbsp extra-virgin olive oil

Add and cook, stirring, until beginning to colour, about 10 minutes:

1 medium red onion, coarsely chopped
Salt and ground black pepper to taste

Meanwhile, rub the bread on both sides with:

1 clove garlic, halved

Coarsely chop together:

4 large cloves garlic, peeled
5 tbsp fresh basil leaves

Reduce the heat to medium-low, stir in the garlic mixture, and cook until the garlic barely colours, 2 to 3 minutes. Add:

750g (1½ lb) ripe tomatoes, peeled, seeded and coarsely chopped, or two 400g (14oz)
tins whole tomatoes, drained and chopped
Pinch of crushed chilli flakes

Cook, stirring, over medium-high heat until thick and fragrant, about 5 minutes. Stir in:

500ml (16floz) *Chicken Stock*, 22, or *Vegetable Stock*, 20

Boil for 2 minutes. Taste and adjust the seasonings. Break up the bread in the bottom of soup bowls. Ladle in the hot soup and top each serving with:

4 fresh basil leaves, torn
Drizzle of extra-virgin olive oil
Parmesan cheese shavings

Serve hot or at room temperature.

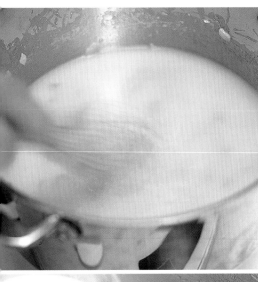

Cheddar Cheese Soup

About 1.5 litres (2½ pints)

Serve this soup as a main course.
Melt in a soup pot, over medium heat:

90g (3oz) unsalted butter

Add and cook until tender, but not browned, 5 to 10 minutes:

125g (4oz) diced onions
125g (4oz) diced celery
125g (4oz) diced carrots

Sprinkle with:

4 tbsp plain flour

Cook, stirring, for 3 to 4 minutes more. Slowly whisk in:

1 litre (1½ pints) *Chicken Stock*, 22

Bring the soup to a boil, whisking constantly. Reduce the heat to a simmer and cook until thickened, about 45 minutes. Purée until smooth. Return to the pot, bring to a simmer and stir in:

250ml (8floz) double or single cream
250g (8oz) Cheddar cheese, grated
1 tsp mustard powder

Reduce the heat to low and stir until the cheese is melted. (Do not let the soup boil: if the soup is too hot, the cheese will break down.) Season with:

Tabasco sauce to taste (optional)
Worcestershire sauce to taste (optional)
Salt and ground black pepper to taste

If you prefer a thinner soup, thin with additional:

Stock or cream

Garnish with:

Croutons, 124
Finely chopped smoked ham
Chopped cooked broccoli

French Onion Soup

About 2 litres (3¼ pints)

The secret to this beloved classic is long, slow cooking of the onions to allow their natural sugars to caramelize; this gives the soup its characteristic depth of flavour and rich mahogany colour.

Heat in a soup pot over medium-low heat until the butter is melted:

30g (1oz) unsalted butter
2 tbsp olive oil

Add and stir to coat:

5 medium onions, thinly sliced
Pinch of dried thyme

Cook, stirring occasionally, and keeping a vigilant eye on the onions so they do not scorch, over medium heat. As soon as they start to brown, after about 15 minutes, reduce the heat to medium-low and continue to cook, covered, stirring more often, until the onions are a rich brown colour, about 40 minutes. Stir in:

2 tbsp dry sherry or cognac

Increase the heat to high and cook, stirring constantly, until all the sherry has cooked off. Stir in:

875ml (1½ pints) *Brown Beef Stock*, 24, *Roasted Vegetable Stock*, 20, or *Brown Chicken Stock*, 22

Bring to a boil, reduce the heat and simmer, partially covered, for 20 minutes.

Season with:

1-1½ tsp salt
¼ - ½ tsp ground black pepper

Place 8 ovenproof soup bowls or crocks on a baking tray. Ladle the hot soup into the bowls and top each serving with:

1-3 slices French bread, toasted if fresh

Sprinkle each bowl with:

3 tbsp grated Gruyère cheese

Broil or bake in a 230°C (450°F) Gas 8 oven until the cheese is melted and starting to brown. Serve immediately.

Gazpacho

About 1.5 litres (2½ pints)

There are numerous varieties of gazpacho in Spain – a white one from Málaga, made with garlic, bread and almonds and garnished with green grapes; a cumin-scented one from Granada; even a stewlike game-filled version (called gaspatxos) from Alicante. The familiar version is this one – an Andalusian "puréed salad" of summery vegetables (opposite). Classic gazpachos are thickened with bread, although many contemporary recipes, like this one, omit it. We have added a nontraditional jalapeño pepper for more bite. Gazpacho is better served the day it is made, but if preparing it for the next day, use half the jalapeño, as the heat increases with time.

Finely chop, but do not purée, in a food processor or blender:

1 medium cucumber, peeled, seeded and coarsely chopped

1 medium green pepper, coarsely chopped

Remove to a large bowl. Finely chop in the processor:

1 small onion, coarsely chopped

5 tbsp fresh parsley leaves

Remove to the bowl. Add to the processor and finely chop:

1.25kg (2½ lb) ripe tomatoes, peeled, seeded and coarsely chopped

Remove to the bowl. Add:

250ml (8floz) tomato juice

60ml (2floz) red wine vinegar

3 tbsp extra-virgin olive oil

2 cloves garlic, finely chopped

1 fresh jalapeño pepper, seeded and chopped, or a dash of Tabasco sauce (optional)

2 tsp salt

Stir well. Refrigerate for at least 2 hours. Serve in chilled bowls.

CUCUMBERS

These quenching vegetables – about 96 percent water – are cucurbitas, part of a huge family that includes squashes. They may be field or hothouse grown, long and slender or stubby or round, and nearly seedless or filled with seeds. We eat them when they are green and immature. The round lemon cucumber, however, we eat when mature and pale yellow. Cucumbers' season is summer and early autumn, although they are nearly always in the market. Select cucumbers that are a rich green and sound and firm – no soft spots, bruises or cuts. Usually the smallest cucumbers are the least mature and therefore have the smallest seeds. Store in perforated plastic bags in the refrigerator.

Barbecued Tomato Soup

About 1 litre (1½ pints)

An intensely flavoured soup that is delicious hot or cold. The barbecuing brings out the sweetness of the tomato and adds smoky flavour. If you cannot barbecue the tomatoes, grill them as close as possible to the heating element. The soup may thicken more when it is cold than when it is hot. To thin, add a little more stock or a bit of water.

Preheat the barbecue or grill. Halve through the circumference and seed:

1.5kg (3lb) ripe tomatoes

Brush both sides with:

Olive oil, preferably extra virgin

If barbecuing, simply place on the barbecue. If grilling, arrange skin side up in a roasting tin. Barbecue or grill the tomatoes on both sides until golden and slightly charred. Remove to a platter or leave in the roasting tin. Heat in a soup pot, over medium-low heat:

2 tbsp olive oil, preferably extra virgin

Add and cook, stirring often, until tender but not brown, 5 to 10 minutes:

1 medium onion, coarsely chopped

Add the tomatoes and stir, breaking up the tomatoes with the spoon. Stir in:

250ml (8floz) Chicken Stock, 22

1 tbsp dry white wine

1 clove garlic, finely chopped

Simmer until the tomatoes are softened and have released their juices, 25 to 30 minutes. Purée until smooth. Strain, if you wish, to remove the skin. Stir in:

¾ tsp salt

¼ tsp ground black pepper

Let cool to room temperature and refrigerate until cold. Just before serving, stir in:

2 tbsp fresh lemon juice

1 tsp balsamic vinegar

2 tbsp chopped fresh basil

Adjust the seasonings, ladle into bowls and garnish each with:

1 sprig fresh basil

1 thin slice lemon (optional)

Tomato Jalapeño Chilaquiles

About 1 litre (1½ pints)

Heat a medium, heavy frying pan or griddle (preferably cast iron) over medium heat until hot. Place in the frying pan:

1-2 fresh jalapeño peppers
2 large cloves garlic, unpeeled

Roast, turning occasionally, until the chilli peppers are blistered and blackened on all sides and the garlic is soft to the touch, 10 to 15 minutes. When cool enough to handle, peel the garlic. Place in a food processor or blender with the chilli peppers. Coarsely chop using on-off pulses. Add:

Two 400g (14oz) tins whole
**   tomatoes, drained**

Process until the mixture is coarsely puréed. Heat in a soup pot over medium heat:

1½ tsp vegetable oil

Add and cook until nicely browned, about 8 to 10 minutes:

½ small onion, thinly sliced

Increase the heat to medium-high and add the tomato mixture. Cook, stirring, until the mixture is darkened and slightly thickened, about 5 minutes. Reduce the heat to medium-low and stir in:

750ml (24floz) Chicken Stock, 22,
**   Chicken Broth, 29, Vegetable Stock, 20,**
**   or Vegetable Broth, 29**

Simmer, stirring occasionally, for 15 minutes. Season with:

½ -1 tsp salt (depending on the
**   saltiness of the broth)**

Just before serving, bring the mixture to a boil and add:

250g (8oz) thick homemade-style
**   tortilla chips**

Stir to coat the chips well, then increase the heat to medium-high and boil rapidly, stirring gently and often, until the chips are softened (but are still a little chewy) and the sauce is reduced to a medium-thick consistency, 2 to 3 minutes for thinner chips, 4 to 5 minutes for thicker chips. Immediately spoon the *chilaquiles* onto a warm deep platter. Serve garnished with:

4 tbsp finely crumbled queso
**   fresco or grated mild Cheddar**
2 tbsp chopped fresh coriander
**   (optional)**
2 tbsp sour cream thinned with a
**   little milk (optional)**

Okra Stew

4 to 6 servings

In this recipe, okra is kept whole to reduce its thickening effect. Soaking okra in vinegar helps reduce its sticky juices even further. Do not cook this stew in an aluminium, iron or unlined copper pot – these metals react with okra. This stew is delicious served over cooked rice.

Combine in a bowl and marinate for 30 minutes:

500g (1lb) fresh or thawed frozen
**   whole okra, stems trimmed**
125ml (4floz) red wine vinegar
2 tbsp salt

Drain and rinse under cold running water. Heat in a large frying pan over medium heat:

3 tbsp olive or vegetable oil

Add:

2 onions, chopped
2 cloves garlic, finely chopped

Cook until lightly coloured around the edges, 4 to 5 minutes. Add:

500g (1lb) fresh or tinned
**   tomatoes, peeled, seeded**
**   and diced**
1 tsp sugar

Cook over medium-low heat until thick, about 30 minutes. Add the okra and season with:

Salt and ground black pepper
**   to taste**

Cook until the okra is tender, about 10 minutes more. Serve in bowls.

OKRA

Okra pods are the young seedpods of a beautiful plant related to hollyhocks and hibiscus. Whole pods, untouched by a knife, are steamed or sautéed for just 3 to 5 minutes. The pods emerge tender but still crisp. The pods are not gummy. When desired, the pods can be cut into thick slices so they can release their sweet mucilaginous ingredient for a natural thickening. The secret to superb eating is to choose pods no longer than your little finger. Pods should be heavy for their size, moist and plump, blemish free, with stems intact.

Cold Avocado Soup

About 1 litre (1½ pints)

Flavourful ripe Haas avocados, the kind with the bumpy skins, are best for this colourful summer soup.

Purée in a food processor or food mill until smooth:

2 ripe avocados (about 500g/1lb), peeled and stoned

1 small clove garlic, chopped

Stir in:

500ml (16floz) buttermilk

4 tsp fresh lime juice

¼ tsp salt

Pinch of cayenne pepper

Remove to a bowl and refrigerate until cold. Thin, if necessary, with:

60-125ml (2-4floz) buttermilk or water

Taste and adjust the seasonings. Ladle the soup into chilled bowls and garnish with:

375ml (12floz) *Salsa Fresca*, 118

2 tbsp sour cream or yoghurt

250g (8oz) fresh lump crabmeat, picked over, or cooked prawns (optional)

AVOCADOS

Grown in warm, sunny countries around the world, avocados are available all year round. The Haas variety is a purplish black, pebbly skinned avocado of the Guatemalan type. Haas avocados weigh about 250g (8oz) and have superior flavour. Their flesh is so rich and buttery because it contains twice as much fat as the smaller, smooth-skinned, green Mexican type of avocados. Another avocado, smooth green Fuerte, is probably a Guatemalan-Mexican hybrid. Although fat means calories, most fat in avocados is mono-unsaturated, the friendly sort found in olives. From southern Florida and Hawaii also comes the yellow-skinned West Indian avocado. Should you find 30-60g (1-2oz) cocktail avocados (they are Fuertes or Mexican fruits with no seed, remnants of dropped pollinated flowers), prepare as you would for any other type of avocado.

Choose an unblemished fruit that is heavy for its size, ideally one that is tender when gently pressed between your hands. Ripe avocados are rarely found at the supermarket, so plan to buy them about 3 days before you will need them. Until it is cut, a stone-hard avocado will ripen in a brown paper bag kept at room temperature out of the sun in about that much time. Slightly overripe fruit can be used for mashing but not slicing. Refrigerate ripe fruits for up to 2 days. Avocado flesh quickly darkens when exposed to air. This does not affect quality or flavour but mars the beauty of the fruit. To prevent avocados from darkening, immediately rub cut surfaces with a slice of citrus – the more the better. Avocados turn bitter when cooked, so enjoy them raw. When adding avocado to cooked dishes, do it at the last minute, off the heat.

Provençal Vegetable Soup (Soupe au Pistou)

About 2.5 litres (4 pints)

This signature dish of the south of France is a light and flavourful vegetable soup (opposite).

Heat in a large soup pot, over medium-low heat:

2 tbsp olive oil, preferably extra-virgin

Add and cook, stirring, until tender but not browned, 5 to 10 minutes:

1 medium onion, chopped
1 small leek (white and tender green parts), cleaned thoroughly and chopped
1 medium carrot, peeled and chopped
1 large celery stalk, chopped

Stir in:

2 medium, ripe tomatoes, peeled, seeded and chopped
1 small potato, peeled and chopped
2 litres (3¼ pints) water
2 tsp salt
Pinch of saffron threads (optional)

Bring to a boil, reduce the heat, and simmer until the potatoes are tender, about 30 minutes. Stir in:

400g (14oz) tin cannellini beans, rinsed and drained, or 185-375g (6-12oz) cooked, 67
Small handful of thin spaghetti, broken up, or short macaroni
1 small courgette, quartered lengthwise and sliced
125g (4oz) green beans, cut into 2.5cm (1in) pieces

Simmer just until the pasta is tender. Meanwhile, make the pistou. Purée in a blender, until smooth:

60g (2oz) fresh basil leaves
2 cloves garlic, chopped
60ml (2floz) extra-virgin olive oil

Remove the soup from the heat. Immediately stir in the pistou along with:

60g (2oz) coarsely grated Parmesan cheese
1 tsp ground black pepper

Ladle into warmed bowls to serve hot, or serve at room temperature or cold.

Roast Red Pepper Soup

About 2 litres (3¼ pints)

This is a rustic-style soup that is full of texture and sweet red pepper flavour. If fresh fennel is not available, use an equal amount of chopped celery and increase the fennel seeds to 1¼ tsp. Serve either hot or cold with grilled garlic toasts.

Preheat the grill.

Arrange skin side up in a roasting tin:

6 large red peppers, quartered and seeded

Trim if necessary so the peppers lie flat and brush them lightly with:

Olive oil

Place under the grill and cook until the skins are thoroughly blistered and blackened. Remove the tin to a rack. When cool enough to handle, peel the peppers, discarding the skins, and cut into long strips. Heat in a soup pot over medium-low heat:

3 tbsp olive oil

Add and cook, stirring, until tender but not browned, 10 to 15 minutes:

250g (8oz) chopped onions
185g (6oz) diced carrots
125g (4oz) chopped fennel bulb

Stir in:

1.25 litres (2 pints) *Chicken Stock*, 22, or *Vegetable Stock*, 20
250ml (8floz) dry white wine
3 tbsp medium-grain rice, preferably Arborio
2 tbsp chopped fresh basil, or 2 tsp dried
1 tbsp chopped fresh rosemary, or 1 tsp dried
1 tsp fennel seeds
⅛ tsp crushed chilli flakes

Bring to a boil, reduce the heat and simmer partially covered, until the peppers and rice are very tender, about 30 minutes. Meanwhile, make the garlic toasts. Preheat the grill. Arrange on a baking tray:

8 slices Italian bread or 16 slices French bread

Lightly brush the slices on both sides with:

Olive oil, preferably extra-virgin

Rub on both sides with:

1-2 cloves garlic, halved

Grill the bread on both sides until golden. When the soup is done, purée until smooth. Return the soup to the pot and season with:

Salt and ground black pepper to taste
2-3 drops balsamic vinegar

Ladle into bowls or let cool to room temperature and refrigerate. Serve with the garlic toasts. If serving chilled, taste cold and adjust the seasonings.

Portuguese Greens Soup (Caldo Verde)

About 2.5 litres (4 pints)

This hearty soup is from the province of Minho, Portugal, which is famous for its cooking.

Heat in a large soup pot, over medium-low heat:

1½ tbsp olive or other vegetable oil

Add and cook, stirring, until tender but not browned, 5 to 10 minutes:

1 medium onion, chopped
2 cloves garlic, finely chopped

Stir in:

2 litres (3¼ pints) water, or
1.5 litres (2½ pints) water and
500ml (16floz) Chicken Stock, 22
4 medium potatoes, peeled and thinly sliced
1½ tsp salt
½ tsp ground black pepper

Bring to a boil, reduce the heat and simmer until the potatoes are soft, about 20 minutes. Remove the pot from the heat. Using a potato masher, lightly mash the potatoes right in the pot. (This will give the soup a chunky texture.) Heat in a medium frying pan, over medium-high heat:

½ tsp vegetable oil (optional)

Add and cook, stirring, until browned:

185g (6oz) Portuguese linguiça or chorizo sausage, thinly sliced

Add to the soup pot. Pour 250ml (8floz) of the soup into the pan. Scrape up the browned bits and return the liquid and browned bits to the soup. Simmer for 5 minutes. Stir in:

250g (8oz) shredded kale, Swiss chard or collard leaves, washed and dried

Simmer for 5 minutes. Stir in:

2 tbsp fresh lemon juice

Ladle into warmed bowls.

KALE, SWISS CHARD AND COLLARD GREENS

Kale (left) deserves to be appreciated as much as spinach. Most culinary kales have blue, magenta or greyish leaves that are curled, crinkly or deeply cut. Their leaves have a delicate cabbage taste and are sweetest when grown in cold climates and picked after a frost.

When you see the large, ruffled, rich green leaves of Swiss chard in the market, you might imagine they have a flamboyant flavour to match. In fact, chard has a more delicate taste than spinach, and very young chard leaves are as mild as lettuce. The Swiss is a puzzlement; there is nothing Swiss about this close relative of beetroot. Chard leaves may be green with white ribs or burgundy with crimson ribs. (Burgundy-coloured chard is also known as rhubarb chard.) But there is more to this vegetable than leaves. The fleshy ribs can be prepared separately; they taste like earthy celery.

Collard's large, smooth, dark green leaves have a flavour somewhere between cabbage or kale and turnip greens, fellow members of the mustard family. Depending on their size and age, they can be mild and sweet or mustardy. Collards do not form a head but grow on stalks that are too tough to eat. The leaves cook fairly quickly.

Select bunches of kale, Swiss chard and collard greens with the crispest, brightest leaves and no yellowing, tears or holes. Store in perforated plastic vegetable bags in the refrigerator drawer.

Southeast Asian Curried Vegetable Stew

6 servings

Heat in a wok or large saucepan over medium heat:

1 tbsp vegetable oil

Add:

1½ tsp cumin seeds

Cook, stirring, for 1 to 2 minutes. Process in a food processor to a smooth paste:

½ medium onion, coarsely chopped

2.5cm (1in) piece fresh ginger, peeled and quartered

4 cloves garlic, peeled

1-2 medium fresh jalapeño peppers, seeded

1 tsp ground turmeric

2 tbsp water

Add the paste to the cumin seeds and cook, stirring often, over medium-low heat for 3 to 5 minutes. Stir in:

400g (14oz) tin unsweetened coconut milk

125ml (4floz) chicken or vegetable stock

500g (1lb) sweet potatoes, peeled and cut into 2cm (¾ in) cubes

Bring to a boil. Reduce the heat and simmer, covered, for 8 minutes. Stir in:

250g (8oz) broccoli florets and cut stems

315g (10½ oz) packet firm tofu, or 250g (8oz) tempeh, cut into 2cm (¾ in) cubes

Simmer, covered, until the broccoli is tender, about 10 minutes. Add and bring to a boil:

1 large tomato, coarsely chopped

Combine and stir in:

3 tbsp fresh lime juice

2 tbsp water

2 tbsp plain flour

Boil, stirring, until thickened, about 1 minute. Stir in:

½ -1 tsp chilli paste

Salt and ground black pepper to taste

Arrange on a serving platter:

1kg (2lb) hot cooked brown or white rice

Spoon the vegetable curry over the rice and sprinkle generously with:

Finely chopped fresh coriander

Chopped cashews (optional)

Root Vegetable and Seitan Stew

8 servings

Vary the vegetables for the stew depending upon availability and preference. Turnips, swedes, sweet potatoes, kohlrabi and fennel are other delicious choices.

Heat in a large flameproof casserole or heavy pot over low heat:

2 tbsp vegetable oil

Add:

125g (4oz) sliced onions
90g (3oz) sliced leeks
   (white part only)
185g (6oz) sliced peeled carrots
5 cloves garlic, finely chopped

Cook, covered, stirring occasionally, until very soft, about 20 minutes. Stir in:

1 tbsp sugar

Cook, uncovered, stirring occasionally, over medium to medium-low heat until the onions are caramelized, 10 to 15 minutes. Stir in:

500g (1lb) chopped mixed
   mushrooms, such as portobello,
   shiitake and/or oyster

Cook for 3 to 4 minutes, then stir in:

3 tbsp plain flour

Cook for 1 minute. Cut into 2-2.5cm (¾-1in) cubes and add:

1 medium baking potato
1 medium parsnip, peeled
1 small butternut squash, peeled
   and seeded

Stir in:

625ml (1 pint) *Vegetable Stock*, 20
125ml (4floz) dry white wine or
   vegetable stock
½ tsp dried rosemary
½ tsp dried thyme
2 or 3 pinches of freshly grated or
   ground nutmeg

Bring to a boil. Reduce the heat and simmer, covered, for 20 minutes. Stir in:

185g (6oz) halved small
   Brussels sprouts
185g (6oz) chopped plum tomatoes
250g (8oz) chopped unpeeled
   Jerusalem artichokes
500g (1lb) seitan, cut into 2.5cm
   (1in) cubes

Simmer, covered, for 20 minutes more. Season with:

Salt and ground black pepper
   to taste

If desired, serve over:

Hot cooked bulgur or brown rice

SEITAN

Also called wheat gluten or wheat meat, seitan is a protein-rich Oriental meat substitute, but one that uses wheat instead of soy (as tofu does). It was invented by Buddhist monks centuries ago to bring the texture and protein of meat to their vegetarian diet. Seitan is made by kneading and washing a dough of very high protein flour to develop the wheat's gluten and remove its starch and bran. Shaped into chunks, balls, cutlets or a large sausage, the greyish gluten is then simmered gently in stock for several hours. It swells, absorbs flavour and becomes firm with cooking.

You can shortcut the tricky process of making seitan at home by starting with a packaged mix or buying ready-to-use seitan in jars or refrigerated tubs or packages. Check the expiry date on refrigerated seitan; refrigerate for no longer than a week after opening or freeze it for 3 to 4 weeks. Ready-made seitan is sold in the stock it was cooked in, which may be flavoured with soy sauce and ginger or with Mexican, Italian, Thai or other seasonings.

Seitan can be prepared in any way that will disguise its greyness but should not be cooked much longer than necessary to heat and sauce it thoroughly, as lengthy cooking brings out a bitter taste. It is a nice addition to quick-cooking stews.

Seitan provides 16 grams protein per 125g (4oz) serving, has no fat, and is rich in iron. Keep in mind that seitan should be avoided by anyone sensitive to gluten, especially those with celiac disease.

ABOUT
PULSE
SOUPS & STEWS

For the contemporary cook, pulse soups and stews have many advantages, besides their great nutrition: they are easy to prepare in large batches, they freeze well, the raw materials are easily kept on hand and they require little attention while cooking.

Puréed bean soups can be passed through a sieve or food mill to eliminate the skins. If a pulse soup or stew becomes too thick during long simmering, simply thin it with a bit of water or stock. Do not purée for a chunkier soup.

Cuban Black Bean Soup (Sopa de Frijol Negro), 70

Soaking Beans

Whether or not to soak beans before cooking is a hot topic today. Many noted food professionals argue that fresh dried beans do not benefit from presoaking before cooking. Heating the pulses to boiling and then simmering them until they swell with water and soften can be done in one continuous process. In order to ensure success with this method, the beans must be of high quality and fresh. Given the limited availability of high-quality fresh dried beans, presoaking the beans first is kinder, both to the bean and to the cook. Not only does it save anywhere from 30 minutes to over an hour on the stove, but it also treats the seed coat more gently than steady simmering, so that the shape of the bean holds without breaking. At high elevations, where simmering times will be extended by the lower temperature of the boiling water, soaking for up to 24 hours is good time-saving insurance.

Before you prepare any pulses, spread them in a pan or large colander and remove any tiny stones that may have accompanied them out of the field. Then rinse the beans very well under cold water, raking them with your fingers to get rid of any clumps of dirt.

Our preferred soaking method is to heat the soaking water, which hastens the swelling of the beans. For a gentle quick-soak, pour boiling water over the beans to cover by 5cm (2in), cover, let stand until the beans have swelled to at least twice their size and have absorbed most of the water, and then drain, discarding the soaking liquid. This will take at least an hour and possibly longer, but the beans will remain firm and keep their shape when cooked.

Another way to soak beans is to place them in a large bowl or pot and add water to cover by at least 5cm (2in). Cover and let stand for up to 24 hours; refrigerate to prevent fermentation if the kitchen is very warm. The beans will swell to triple their dried size. Drain well and discard the soaking liquid.

A third method, which risks breaking some bean skins, is to place the beans in a saucepan, add water to cover by 5cm (2in), and heat to boiling; then reduce the heat and simmer for 2 minutes. Let stand, covered, for 1 hour. Or microwave 500g (1lb) beans and 1 litre (1½ pints) water in a covered 3-4 litre (5-6 pint) casserole on high to boiling, 12 to 17 minutes, and then on medium for 2 minutes. Stir and let stand, covered, for 1 hour. With all three soaking methods, be sure to rinse and drain the beans before the final cooking.

Cooking Beans

To cook beans, place them in a large pot and add cold water to cover by 5cm (2in). Bring to a boil over high heat; skim off the foam that rises to the surface. Reduce the heat to low and cover; simmer, stirring and skimming occasionally, until the beans are tender. Do not boil rapidly or the abrasion will loosen the bean skins. If the pot threatens to boil over, partially remove the cover. Cook beans uncovered if you have seasoned the liquid and want some of it to evaporate to concentrate the flavour or to thicken the dish. Baking is an alternative to boiling, especially with black, red and white beans; the benefits are better shape and creamier texture.

Beans readily absorb seasonings from water. A classic way to add flavour is to bury one or two smoked ham knuckles or a ham bone in the beans; smoked turkey can be substituted. Add a couple of bay leaves and an onion studded with a half-dozen cloves to the ham or turkey, and the beans will taste smoky and slightly spicy. Simmer beans with chopped onions and carrots to sweeten them; use at least 125g (4oz) of each with 500g (1lb) of beans, because the water will dilute their impact. Whole allspice and a piece of cinnamon stick are especially good with black or red beans; wrap spices in muslin or place in a tea ball for easy removal. Whole bay leaves and dried thyme or rosemary bring nice herbal notes to white and lima beans. The possibilities are infinite and come with only a few caveats. First, expect that any salty ingredients, such as smoked meats, will slow the cooking a little; do not add plain salt until near the end, when the beans have already softened. Do not add tomatoes, citrus, vinegar, molasses or any other acidic ingredients until near the end, after the beans are tender; acid, like salt, prevents the beans from softening. This principle is conveniently applied in reverse when you make Boston baked beans: the precooked beans do not turn mushy when baked for hours because the added molasses and tomatoes keep the skins firm.

If you want relatively firm beans to use in recipes that call for further cooking without acidic ingredients, remove a few beans and pinch them for tenderness at the low end of the cooking time range. If you want very soft beans for a soup or stew, you may decide to cook them longer than suggested. If so, be sure there is enough water in the pot to keep the beans from drying out. Add more as needed, for the beans will not continue to soften without more water to absorb.

Tinned beans can be substituted weight for weight in recipes that call for cooked beans, but they are almost always softer and less flavourful. Since brands vary in quality, it is worth trying different ones. Rinsing tinned beans improves the taste a little and removes excess salt. To rinse well, put the beans in a large sieve set in a pot or bowl and let cold water run over the beans until the pot is filled, raking the beans with your fingers, and drain, repeat, and then drain well.

Lentil Soup

About 2.5 litres (4 pints)

Heat in a large soup pot, over medium-low heat:

3 tbsp olive oil

Add and cook, stirring, until tender but not browned, 5 to 10 minutes:

3 medium carrots, peeled and diced
3 medium celery stalks, diced
1 large onion, diced
3 cloves garlic, finely chopped

60g (2oz) prosciutto or pancetta, or 4 slices bacon, diced (optional)

Stir in:

2 litres (3¼ pints) water
375g (12oz) lentils, picked over and rinsed
400g (14oz) tin chopped tomatoes, drained

1 tsp dried thyme

Bring to a boil, reduce the heat and simmer until the lentils are tender, 30 to 45 minutes. Stir in:

1½ tsp balsamic vinegar
2 tsp salt (1 tsp if using the meat)
1 tsp ground black pepper

Ladle into warmed bowls.

Split Pea Soup

About 1.5 litres (2½ pints)

Try this soup on a cold winter day, seasoned with plenty of freshly ground black pepper.

Combine in a soup pot:

2 litres (3¼ pints) cold water
1 small ham knuckle
500g (1lb) split green peas

Bring to a boil, reduce the heat, and simmer for 1 hour.

Stir in:

1 large carrot, peeled and diced
1 large celery stalk, diced
1 medium onion, diced
2 cloves garlic, finely chopped
1 Bouquet Garni, 17

Simmer until the ham knuckle and peas are tender, about 1 hour more. Season with:

Salt and lots of ground black pepper to taste

Remove the ham knuckle. Discard the bone, skin and fat; dice the meat. Return it to the soup. For a thicker soup, simmer to the desired consistency. Stir to blend before serving. Ladle into warmed bowls. Garnish with:

Croutons, 124

SPLIT PEAS

Green split peas remind us how good peas taste, with a flavour more intense than that of young green peas and a much denser texture. Yellow split peas are similar but blander, providing a more neutral backdrop for all kinds of seasonings. Both green and yellow split peas cook to a thick, creamy texture that is perfect for soups such as classic split pea. The technique of steaming dried peas to loosen their skins, then peeling and splitting them to hasten cooking, has been practised in India for thousands of years. The resulting products, shiny green and yellow split peas, are so convenient to use that they have largely displaced dried whole peas, with their grey-green skins, on supermarket shelves. There are other advantages to using split peas. Whole dried peas need soaking; split peas do not. Because they have no skins, split peas lose their shape in the pot; for the same reason, they can be cooked with salt, for there are no skins to toughen.

Caribbean Red Bean Stew with Pork

4 to 6 servings

This stew makes a hearty meal.

Pick over, rinse, and soak, 66:

280g (9oz) dried red kidney, pinto or small red beans

Drain. Combine the beans in a large saucepan with:

2 litres (3¼ pints) water
1 small onion
1 leafy celery top
1 bay leaf
1 clove garlic, peeled
7.5cm (3in) cinnamon stick

Bring to a boil. Reduce the heat and simmer, covered, until the beans are tender, about 1 hour. Drain, reserving 1 litre (1½ pints) of the cooking liquid. Discard the vegetables and seasonings. Heat in a large saucepan over medium heat:

1 tbsp olive oil

Add and brown on all sides:

500g (1lb) trimmed boneless pork, cut into 2.5cm (1in) cubes

Add:

1 large onion, cut into 1cm (½ in) cubes
1 green pepper, cut into 2.5cm (1in) pieces

375g (12oz) peeled sweet potato, cut into 2.5cm (1in) cubes
1 tbsp coarsely chopped garlic
1 tsp salt

Cook, stirring, until the onions are golden, 12 to 15 minutes. Add:

2 tsp hot paprika

Stir to blend. Add the cooked beans and the reserved cooking liquid. Bring to a boil. Reduce the heat and simmer, uncovered, until the pork is tender and the stew is thick, about 1 hour. Serve hot.

U.S. Senate Bean Soup

About 1.5 litres (2½ pints)

This soup has been on the U.S. Senate restaurant menu since 1901.

Pick over, rinse and soak, 66:

250g (8oz) small dried white beans, such as haricot or navy

Drain and place in a soup pot along with:

1.75 litres (2¾ pints) cold water

1 small ham knuckle

Bring to a boil, reduce the heat and simmer until the beans are tender, about 1¼ hours. Remove the ham knuckle. Discard the bone, skin and fat; dice the meat. Return it to the pot along with:

1 large onion, diced

3 medium celery stalks with leaves, chopped

1 large potato, peeled and finely diced

2 cloves garlic, finely chopped

1½ tsp salt

½ tsp ground black pepper

Simmer until the potatoes are quite soft, 20 to 30 minutes. Remove from the heat and mash with a potato masher until the soup is a bit creamy. Stir in:

2 tbsp chopped fresh parsley

Ladle into warmed bowls.

Cuban Black Bean Soup (Sopa de Frijol Negro)

About 2 litres (3¼ pints)

Pick over, rinse, and soak, 66:

500g (1lb) dried black beans

Heat in a large soup pot over medium-low heat:

2 tbsp vegetable oil

Add and cook, stirring, until tender but not browned, 5 to 10 minutes:

2 medium onions, chopped

3 medium celery stalks, diced

4 cloves garlic, finely chopped

½ Scotch bonnet chilli or 2-3 fresh jalapeño chilli peppers, seeded and diced

Drain and add the black beans along with:

2.75 litres (4½ pints) water

1 large ham knuckle (optional)

Bring to a boil, reduce the heat, and simmer until the beans are tender, about 2 hours. Remove the ham knuckle if using. Discard the bone, skin and fat; dice the meat. Purée the beans in a food processor or by passing them through a food mill. Return to the pot. Stir in the meat along with:

60-125ml (2-4floz) dry sherry or rum

2 tsp salt (less if using the ham knuckle)

Simmer for several minutes to heat through. Thin with additional water if necessary. Stir in:

2 tbsp fresh lemon juice (optional)

Garnish at the table with any or all of the following:

Lemon wedges

Chopped onions

Steamed white rice

Chopped hard-boiled eggs

Chopped spring onions

Wild Caribbean Black Bean Chilli

8 to 10 servings

To the traditional chilli seasonings of cumin and chilli powder, this Caribbean-inspired black bean version adds the tang of citrus and the blistering floral heat of the habanero chilli. Jalapeño chilli peppers, which can be substituted, vary considerably in their heat from totally mild to quite hot varieties found in some supermarkets.

Pick over and rinse:

750g (1½ lb) dried black beans

Drain. Combine the beans in a large pot with water to cover by 5cm (2in). Bring to a boil. Reduce the heat to low and simmer, partially covered, until almost tender, about 1 hour. Drain. Heat in the same large pot over medium heat until hot but not smoking:

60ml (2floz) vegetable oil

Add:

4 medium onions, finely diced

Cook, stirring occasionally, until just starting to brown, 8 to 10 minutes. Add:

4 tbsp finely chopped garlic
1-2 tbsp chopped habanero chillies or 6-8 tbsp chopped fresh jalapeño chillies

Cook, stirring, for 1 minute. Add, stir together well and bring to a simmer:

4 tbsp chilli powder
4 tbsp ground cumin
2 tbsp sugar
2 tsp salt
2 tsp ground black pepper
3 tsp grated orange zest
375ml (12floz) fresh orange juice
2 tsp grated lime zest
180ml (6floz) fresh lime juice
Two 400g (14oz) tins crushed tomatoes
1.5 litres (2½ pints) water

Stir in the reserved black beans. Return to a simmer, cover and reduce the heat to low. Cook, partially covered, checking occasionally and adding more water as needed, until the beans are just soft to the bite, 1½ to 2 hours. Adjust the seasonings and serve, garnished, if desired, with:

Sour cream
Chopped fresh coriander
Chopped spring onions
Lime wedges for squeezing

HABANERO CHILLI PEPPER

The habanero chilli is reputed to be the hottest of all chillies. These lantern-shaped chilli peppers pack tremendous fruity and floral flavours and aromas, along with an incredible punch. Usually found in markets coloured green, yellow-orange or bright orange, habaneros are sometimes mislabelled as the equally hot but less floral Scotch bonnet. Used extensively in the Yucatán, they have become increasingly popular in salsas, sauces, and condiments. They measure about 4cm (1½ in) long and 4cm (1½ in) wide at the stem end.

Mediterranean White Bean Soup

About 1.5 litres (2½ pints)

Simple and aromatic, this is what used to be called a "pantry soup", because it uses household staples. Feel free to add a touch of extra chopped fresh herbs such as thyme, fennel leaves or sage.

Pick over, rinse, and soak, 66:

185g (6oz) large dried white beans, such as cannellini or butter beans

Drain and place in a soup pot along with:

1.75 litres (2¾ pints) water
¾ tsp dried rosemary
8 cloves garlic, chopped or sliced

Bring to a boil, reduce the heat and simmer until the beans are tender, 1 to 1½ hours. Stir in:

90g (3oz) chopped ripe tomatoes
4 tbsp chopped fresh parsley
60ml (2floz) extra-virgin olive oil
4 tsp red wine vinegar
2 tsp salt
½ tsp ground black pepper

Ladle into warmed bowls.

American Peanut Soup

About 1 litre (1½ pints)

Peanuts are among the many culinary treasures taken to the United States by slaves from Africa. If you are preparing this dish a day or so ahead, use less cayenne pepper and Tabasco sauce, as the heat intensifies over time.

Heat in a soup pot, over medium-low heat until the butter is melted:

30g (1oz) unsalted butter
1 tbsp vegetable oil

Add and cook, stirring, until tender but not browned, about 5 to 10 minutes:

1 small onion, chopped
2 medium celery stalks, chopped

Stir in:

2 tbsp plain flour

Reduce the heat to low and cook, stirring, for 5 minutes. Stir in:

1 litre (1½ pints) Chicken Stock, 22, or Brown Chicken Stock, 22

Simmer, stirring often, until the soup begins to thicken, about 5 minutes. Stir in:

250g (8oz) unsalted smooth peanut butter

60ml (2floz) double or single cream
1½ tsp salt
1 tsp cayenne pepper
1 tsp Tabasco sauce

Heat through but do not boil. Stir in:

2 tsp fresh lemon juice

Ladle into warmed bowls. Garnish with:

3 tbsp chopped dry-roasted peanuts
4 tbsp chopped spring onion greens

Sweet Potato and Peanut Stew

6 servings

Omit the minced beef or turkey for a vegetarian version.

Heat in a large, heavy saucepan over medium-low heat:

60ml (2floz) peanut oil

Add:

1 onion, chopped
1 red or green pepper, chopped
1 fresh jalapeño or serrano chilli, seeded and finely chopped

Cook until the vegetables are tender but not brown, 7 to 10 minutes. Add:

4 cloves garlic, finely chopped
1 tbsp finely chopped peeled fresh ginger

Cook for another 2 to 3 minutes and stir in:

1 tbsp chilli powder
1 tsp ground cumin
½ tsp crushed chilli flakes

Cook for 1 minute and add:

2 sweet potatoes, peeled and cut into 4cm (1½ in) pieces
5 tbsp tomato purée

Salt and ground black pepper to taste

Add enough water to barely cover the vegetables and mix well. Bring to a boil, lower the heat, cover and simmer for 45 minutes, stirring occasionally. While the stew cooks, heat in a medium frying pan over high heat:

1 tsp peanut oil

Add:

375g (12oz) minced beef or turkey

Sauté, turning often, until browned. Transfer to a plate with a slotted spoon and set aside until the stew has cooked for 45 minutes. When ready, add the meat to the stew along with:

2 small courgettes (2.5cm/1in in diameter), trimmed and sliced

Cook for another 15 minutes. Place in a small bowl:

125g (4oz) peanut butter (chunky or smooth), preferably unsalted

Stir in 250ml (8floz) of the stewing liquid until smooth and add the peanut butter mixture to the pot. Mix well and cook another 15 minutes. Season with:

Salt and ground black pepper to taste

Serve plain (opposite) or with:

Hot cooked rice or couscous

SWEET POTATOES

When we say "sweet potatoes", we mean the ones with yellow-grey to brown skin and yellowish to white, dry, mealy flesh. Shape is not an indication of quality. All can be round or torpedo shaped, knobby or sleek. Select firm tubers with bright skin, heavy for their size, free of soft spots, dark spots and mould. Although available year-round, the potatoes are harvested fresh from autumn and through winter. Store sweet potatoes in a cool, dark, dry place.

ABOUT
CHOWDERS

*T*he word chowder *usually conjures up images of a steaming bowl of clam chowder. In nineteenth-century America, "chowder masters", as well as home cooks, prepared versions of the soup for gatherings on the beach or at home.*

The word derives from the French chaudière, *a type of cauldron, but regional chowders have become a culinary tradition. Early American settlers made chowder from household staples: rendered salt pork was simmered in water with local fish or seafood, then thickened with sea biscuits or bread. In the nineteenth century, potatoes replaced the crackers, and milk and cream came to be added to chowder. Other milk chowders then evolved, including sweetcorn chowder. Some chowders omit the milk entirely and are tomato-based.*

New England Clam Chowder, 80

Fresh Corn Chowder

About 1.5 litres (2½ pints)

Place in a soup pot and cook, stirring, over medium-low heat until it releases all of its fat and is beginning to crisp, 10 to 15 minutes:

4 slices bacon, chopped

Leaving the bacon in the pan, spoon off all but 2 tbsp of fat. Add and cook, stirring, until tender and slightly browned, 10 to 15 minutes:

1 small onion, chopped

2 medium celery stalks, diced

Remove the kernels from:

6 small ears sweetcorn

Reserve the kernels and add the cobs to the soup pot along with:

Just over 1 litre (1½ pints) milk

2 medium potatoes, peeled and diced

Push the sweetcorn cobs into the milk to fully submerge them. Bring the milk to a boil. Reduce the heat and simmer, covered, until the potatoes are tender, 10 to 15 minutes. Remove the cobs. Stir in the reserved corn kernels along with:

1½ tsp salt

½ tsp ground white or black pepper

Simmer gently until the sweetcorn is tender, about 5 minutes. With a slotted spoon, remove 375ml (12floz) solids from the soup and purée until smooth. Return to the soup and add:

15g (½ oz) unsalted butter

Let stand until the butter is melted, then stir. Ladle into warmed bowls.

PREPARING SWEETCORN

In our recipes we have adopted the formula of one ear sweetcorn to equal 90g (3oz) kernels.

To remove kernels from the cob, hold the ear firmly with the bottom end placed on a counter or in a shallow soup bowl to keep the kernels from splattering. If you want to retain the shape and texture of the whole kernel, cut straight down the cob with a sharp knife, cutting two or three rows at a time (**1**).

If you are after the inner creaminess of the kernel, cut off just the tops of the kernels. Then, with the back of your knife, scrape down the cob to press out the base of the kernels and the sweetcorn "milk", which gives body and moisture to purées and creamy sweetcorn dishes (**2**).

Corn Chowder with Chilli Peppers

About 1.25 litres (2 pints)

A spicy, meatless corn chowder.
Heat in a soup pot, over medium-low heat until the butter is melted:

15g (½ oz) unsalted butter
1 tbsp vegetable oil

Add and cook, stirring, until tender but not browned, 5 to 10 minutes:

1 medium onion, diced
1 medium poblano chilli pepper, seeded and diced
2 cloves garlic, finely chopped
½ fresh jalapeño chilli pepper, seeded and diced

Stir in:

750ml (24floz) milk
375g (12oz) fresh sweetcorn kernels (from 2-3 ears)

1 tsp salt

Bring to a boil, reduce the heat, and simmer gently until the sweetcorn is tender, about 3 minutes. Stir in:

1 large ripe tomato, peeled, seeded and coarsely chopped

Simmer gently for about 2 minutes to marry the flavours. With a slotted spoon, remove 375ml (12floz) solids from the soup and purée until smooth. Return to the soup. Heat gently just to warm through. Stir in:

1 tbsp chopped fresh coriander

Ladle into warmed bowls. If you like, pass at the table:

Lime wedges

POBLANO CHILLI PEPPER

Dark green, rich-tasting poblanos (also called pasillas) are used extensively throughout Mexico and are gaining in popularity in this country. The pepper's flesh has a compact texture with a good (but varying) amount of heat. Use them roasted and peeled in soups, sauces and stews or whole as an edible vessel. When dried, they usually are known as ancho chillies. Poblanos measure 10-13cm (4-5in) long and about 6cm (2½ in) wide at the stem end, tapering to a sharp point.

Manhattan Clam Chowder

About 2.5 litres (4 pints)

Salt pork, onions, seafood, potatoes and, most of the time, milk make a traditional chowder. Manhattan clam chowder substitutes tomatoes for the milk. Some consider this blasphemy, others say it simply is not chowder, others want nothing else.

Scrub individually with a vegetable brush:

5-6kg (10-12lb) large hard-shell clams, preferably 5-7.5cm (2-3in) across

Place the clams in a sink or large soup pot, cover with cold water, and stir in:

4 tbsp salt

Let stand for 30 minutes to rid the clams of sand. Rinse and drain in a colander. Place the clams in a large soup pot and add:

500ml (16floz) water

Cover and steam over high heat until the clams are completely open, 10 to 15 minutes. Discard any that do not open. Pour the cooking liquid through a fine-mesh sieve and set aside. When the clams are cool enough to handle, remove from the shell and chop finely. Heat in a large frying pan, over medium heat:

1 tbsp vegetable oil

Add and cook, stirring occasionally, until browned:

3 slices bacon, finely chopped

Add and cook, stirring, until tender but not browned, 5 to 10 minutes:

2 medium onions, chopped
½ green pepper, diced
1 large celery stalk, diced

Stir in the reserved cooking liquid along with:

Two 400g (14oz) tins whole plum tomatoes, with juice, chopped
750ml (24floz) *Fish Fumet*, 21, or *Express Fish Broth*, 28

Bring to a boil. Stir in:

500g (1lb) potatoes, peeled and cut into 2.5cm (1in) dice

Reduce the heat to medium-low and simmer until the potatoes are tender, about 20 minutes. Stir in the chopped clams and season with:

½ tsp ground black pepper
2 tbsp chopped fresh parsley

Simmer briefly, then ladle into warmed bowls.

HARD-SHELL CLAMS

There are dozens of types of clams. Hard-shell clams vary more in size and colour than in shape or form. But vary they do, from the tiny cockle (not, strictly speaking, a true clam but close enough for culinary purposes), less than 1cm (½ in) across, to the giant sea clam, which can weigh hundreds of kilos. All have firm, sometimes tough, meat with excellent, briny flavour. And all have the distinct advantage of being essentially free of grit. There is some confusion about nomenclature of hard-shell clams, but the common names relate primarily to size.

Littlenecks, the smallest hard-shell, are under 5cm (2in) across (preferably considerably under). Cherrystones in some areas are 5-7.5cm (2-3in) across, in others up to 10cm (4in). They are excellent for cooking. Mahogany clams are the same size. There are some excellent varieties that are steely grey in colour.

RHODE ISLAND (PORTUGUESE-STYLE) CLAM CHOWDER

As unconventional as Manhattan clam chowder, but very tasty. Prepare Manhattan Clam Chowder, above, substituting 2 tbsp olive oil for the bacon and adding along with the clams 185g (6oz) thinly sliced Portuguese linguiça or chorizo sausage and ¼ to ½ tsp crushed chilli flakes (left). Simmer over low heat for 10 minutes. Ladle into warmed bowls.

Landlubber's Fish Chowder

8 to 10 servings

Use salmon, monkfish, blackfish or cod in this fish chowder. Flaky fish, such as flounder, mackerel or sea bass tend to fall apart too easily. Serve as a main course for lunch or dinner. For a reduced-fat fish chowder, omit the cream.

Remove any excess skin and, using tweezers, pick out any bones from:

1.75kg (3½ lb) boneless, skinless fish fillets

If you have to use a knife to cut out the bones, be sure to leave the fillets in pieces as large as possible. Place in a large soup pot and cook, stirring, over low heat until it is beginning to crisp, 10 to 15 minutes:

125g (4oz) meaty salt pork or 4 slices bacon, cut into 5-10mm (¼ - ½ in) dice

Add and cook, stirring, until the onions are tender but not browned, 10 to 15 minutes:

60g (2oz) unsalted butter
2 large onions, cut into 2.5cm (1in) dice
3 bay leaves
1 tbsp chopped fresh thyme

Stir in:

3 large boiling potatoes, peeled, halved lengthwise and cut into 5mm (¼ in) slices
750ml (24floz) Fish Stock, 21, Fish Fumet, 21, or Express Fish Broth, 28

Bring to a boil, reduce the heat and simmer until the potatoes are tender, about 20 minutes. Remove the bay leaves and stir in the fish fillets along with:

500ml (16floz) double cream

Simmer until the fish is cooked through and beginning to flake, 8 to 10 minutes. Season with:

Salt and ground black pepper to taste
2 tbsp chopped fresh parsley and/or chervil

Remove from the heat. Ladle into soup dishes. Top each serving with:

Dollop of butter

Serve with:

Cream Biscuits, 123, or common crackers

New England Clam Chowder

About 1 litre (1½ pints)

This New England clam chowder gets its creamy thickness from double cream and the starch in the potatoes.

Scrub individually with a vegetable brush:

2.5kg (5lb) large hard-shell clams

Place in a sink or large soup pot, cover with cold water, and stir in:

4 tbsp salt

Let stand for 30 minutes to rid the clams of sand. Rinse and drain in a colander. Place the clams in a large soup pot and add:

250ml (8floz) water
Any scraps of onion, celery, thyme or bay leaf (optional)

Cover and steam over high heat until the clams are completely open,

10 to 15 minutes. Discard any that do not open. Pour the cooking liquid through a fine-mesh sieve and set aside. When the clams are cool enough to handle, remove from their shells and coarsely chop into 1cm (½ in) pieces.

Place in a soup pot and cook, stirring, over medium heat until slightly crisp:

2 slices bacon or 60g (2oz) salt pork, diced

Stir in:

1 medium onion, cut into 1cm (½ in) dice
1 bay leaf
1½ tsp chopped fresh thyme
15g (½ oz) unsalted butter

When the onions are translucent, add the reserved cooking liquid along with:

3 red or white new potatoes, cut into 1cm (½ in) dice

Bring to a boil, reduce the heat and simmer until the potatoes are tender, about 12 minutes. Stir in the chopped clams along with:

250ml (8floz) double cream

Simmer for 5 minutes. Season the chowder with:

Ground black pepper to taste
1 tbsp chopped fresh parsley

Ladle into soup dishes or cups. Serve with:

Cream Biscuits, 123, or common crackers

Pacific Northwest Salmon Chowder

About 1.25 litres (2 pints)

In a small saucepan, simmer, whisking occasionally, until reduced to 160ml (5floz):

250ml (8floz) double cream

Meanwhile, melt in a soup pot over medium heat:

15g (½ oz) unsalted butter

Add and cook, stirring, until the leeks are tender but not browned, 5 to 10 minutes:

2 medium leeks (white part only), cleaned and chopped

60ml (2floz) dry vermouth
1 clove garlic, finely chopped

Stir in:

750ml (24floz) Fish Stock, 21, Fish Fumet, 21, or Express Fish Broth, 28
2 red or white new potatoes, diced
½ tsp salt

Bring to a boil, reduce the heat, and simmer until the potatoes are cooked, 10 to 15 minutes. Reduce the heat to low. Add the reduced cream along with:

1 salmon fillet (about 375g/12oz)
¼ tsp ground black or white pepper

Simmer just until the salmon is cooked, 8 to 10 minutes, depending on the thickness of the fish. Gently break apart the fillet with a wooden spoon. Serve immediately, garnished with:

Small dill sprigs

ABOUT
FISH AND
SEAFOOD
SOUPS & STEWS

*F*ish and seafood lend themselves to soups and stews, because they stay moist and tender when cooked at a low temperature and closely watched. But they are easy to overcook, so serve or remove from the heat as soon as the fish is cooked. A light chicken stock is often a better substitute for fish fumet than many commercial fish or clam broths, which may add a fishy taste to the soup. With the exception of most chowders, which tend to sit well overnight, generally fish soups are best eaten as soon as they are cooked.

Bouillabaisse, 86

Cream of Mussel Soup (Billi Bi)

About 1 litre (1½ pints)

This is a French mussel soup made with cream and white wine. The secret to this soup is to strain the mussel cooking liquid through several layers of muslin to make sure you trap every possible grain of sand. You will find the optional curry powder at the end to be a perfect accent against the creamy broth.

Scrub individually with a vegetable brush:

1.5kg (3lb) small mussels

Remove the beards. Discard any damaged mussels or those that do not close with a sharp tap on the counter. Place the mussels in a large soup pot along with:

375ml (12floz) dry white wine
5 tbsp chopped shallots
5 sprigs fresh parsley
3 sprigs fresh thyme

Cover and steam over medium heat until the mussels are completely open. Discard any that do not open. Pour the cooking liquid through a sieve lined with several layers of dampened muslin or paper towels into a medium saucepan. Bring to a low simmer. When the mussels are cool enough to handle, remove from their shells. Whisk together in a small bowl:

250ml (8floz) double or single cream
1 large egg yolk

Gradually whisk about 250ml (8floz) of the cooking liquid into the egg mixture, then whisk back into the saucepan. Heat gently, but do not boil. Season with:

Salt to taste
Pinch of ground red or white pepper
½ tsp curry powder (optional)

Ladle into warmed bowls. Garnish with the reserved mussels and sprinkle with:

Snipped fresh chives

MUSSELS

Blue mussels are the most common variety. New Zealand green-lipped mussels are also good and can be used interchangeably. The quality of mussels is difficult to judge in the shop, and their meat is firm, plump, large, sweet and clean at its best. You can be certain you are buying live mussels, but you cannot be certain you are buying delicious ones. A wise policy is to identify the source when you have good mussels and try to stay with it. Many retailers buy their mussels from the same source over and over again, and they can be consistently fine. Some mussels are farm-raised, and their advocates claim that these are more consistent than wild mussels. Some mussel shells are beautifully clean and shiny; others are encrusted with barnacles and other evidence of life at sea. Neither is an indication of quality. Like clams and oysters, mussels must be alive (or cooked) at the time of purchase. The smell should be appealing and the shell intact. Reject any with broken shells or those that seem unusually light or heavy (they may be empty or filled with mud). Gaping is fine, but live mussels will close, slowly but surely, when you tap the shell.

To clean mussels, remove the "beard", the hairy vegetative growth attached to the shell. You can usually just tug it off or cut it with a knife. Wash the mussels in several changes of cold water (if time allows, place them in a pot and run a slow stream of cold water over them for an hour, no longer). Keep washing until the water runs clear. Sort through the mussels and discard any with damaged shells. Be sure not to store mussels in a sealed plastic bag. They will suffocate. Store preferably in a bowl or mesh bag, in the refrigerator, covered lightly with a damp towel. Ice is not necessary; molluscs will stay alive for days at 4°C (40°F).

Oyster Stew

About 1 litre (1 ½ pints)

This dish comes together quickly. A double boiler prevents overcooking of the oysters. In many American homes, this is often served before the turkey at Thanksgiving, but there is no need to wait for a celebration to enjoy this stew.

Combine in the top of a double boiler set directly over medium-low heat:

30-60g (1-2oz) unsalted butter

1 tbsp or more grated onions or leeks, a sliver of garlic or 90g (3oz) finely chopped celery

Cook, stirring, until the butter is melted and the onions are tender but not browned, about 5 minutes. Stir in:

25-35 shelled oysters, with their liquor

375ml (12floz) milk

125ml (4floz) single cream

½ tsp salt

⅛ tsp ground white pepper or sweet or hot paprika

Place the top of the double boiler over, not in, boiling water. When the milk is hot and the oysters are floating, stir in:

2 tbsp chopped fresh parsley

Ladle into warmed bowls.

OYSTER BISQUE

This is a delicious bisque for oyster lovers. Temper the egg yolks to prevent them from scrambling with a small amount of the stew before adding them to the pot.

Prepare *Oyster Stew, left,* but before adding the parsley, remove the stew from the heat and pour a small quantity over 2 beaten egg yolks. After mixing, add them slowly to the hot stew. Heat over low heat for 1 minute, but do not allow to boil. Serve immediately.

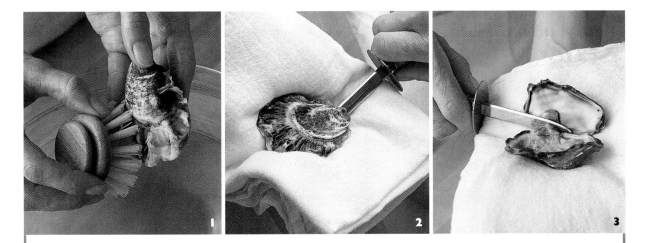

HOW TO CLEAN AND SHUCK OYSTERS

1 To clean oysters, use a stiff brush and scrub the shells thoroughly, in particular the often-encrusted native oysters (Pacific oysters tend to be cleaner).

2 To shuck, or shell, oysters, hold the oyster, deep shell down, firmly in a folded tea towel over a bowl. Insert the point of an oyster knife, which has a strong pointed blade and protective shield, into the hinge between the shells at the pointed end of the oyster. Turn the knife to prise open the oyster and lift the upper shell enough to cut through the hinge muscle. Run the knife point between the shells to open the oyster.

3 Once open, scrape the oyster from its shell, but do not remove it. To serve the oysters raw, nestle the shells in some ice or rock salt. Strain any liquor (oyster liquid) in the bowl and pour it over the oysters. To cook the oysters, remove them to a bowl. Strain the liquor and reserve it for cooking.

Bouillabaisse

4 to 6 servings

In this classic Provençal fisherman's stew, the only rule is that it should be a mix of different kinds of fish and shellfish paired with a combination of garlic, tomato, saffron and fennel. The seafood suggestions in this recipe are only a guide. Well-scrubbed clams, mussels, prawns, all in the shell, can be added, as can a number of fish types such as snapper, halibut and perch. Remember that bouillabaisse should capture the flavour of the freshest catch of the day, and need not adhere to strict rules.

Heat in a large saucepan, over medium heat until the butter is melted:

1 tbsp olive oil

15g (½ oz) unsalted butter

Add and cook, stirring occasionally, until the vegetables are tender but not browned, 5 to 10 minutes:

1 medium leek (white and green parts), cleaned thoroughly, halved lengthwise, and cut into 1cm (½ in) pieces

1 small fennel bulb, quartered, cored and thinly sliced

1 medium celery stalk, cut into thin diagonal slices

1 bay leaf

1 star anise, or ¼ tsp anise seeds or fennel seeds (optional)

Peel of ½ orange (optional)

¼ tsp saffron threads

½ tsp salt

Add:

3 cloves garlic, finely chopped

Cook, stirring, for 2 minutes more. Reduce the heat if the bottom begins to scorch. Add:

1 tbsp tomato purée

Cook, stirring, for 1 minute. Stir in:

125ml (4floz) dry white wine

Bring to a gentle boil and cook for 3 minutes. Stir in:

375ml (12floz) tinned whole tomatoes, with juice, broken into pieces

500ml (16floz) Fish Stock, 21, Fish Fumet, 21, or Express Fish Broth, 28

½ tsp cayenne pepper

¾ tsp salt

Bring to a boil, reduce the heat, cover, and simmer for 20 minutes.

The bouillabaisse broth can be made a day in advance. Bring to the smoking point in a large soup pot over high heat:

2 tbsp olive oil

Add:

12 small hard-shell clams, well scrubbed

Cook, stirring, for 2 to 3 minutes. Keep the oil from smoking. Remove the star anise and orange peel if using, and add the reserved broth. Bring to a boil, reduce the heat and simmer for 3 minutes. Stir in:

375g (12oz) monkfish, sea bass, red snapper or halibut fillets or a combination, cut into 4cm (1½ in) pieces

Continue to cook, covered, for 1 minute. Stir in:

12 large scallops

Cook just until the seafood is done, 2 to 3 minutes more. Discard any clams that are not open. Stir in:

2 tbsp Pernod (optional)

Serve with:

Croutons, 124

Saffron Garlic Mayonnaise, 119

Bourride of Monkfish and Clams

About 2 litres (3¼ pints)

This is a modern take on the classic fish soup from Provence. In honouring the dish's origins, we have stirred the local mayonnaise (aïoli) right into the fish broth. This is an easy dish to prepare and a great dish for entertaining. Shell the clams for a more elegant presentation or arrange them in their shells over the top of the bourride.

Heat in a large nonreactive frying pan over medium-high heat:

60ml (2floz) olive oil

Have ready:

1kg (2lb) monkfish fillets, cut into 5 x 2.5cm (2 x 1in) pieces

Sprinkle with:

Ground black pepper to taste

Place the fish in the frying pan in an even layer and cook until browned on one side, 5 to 7 minutes. Turn the monkfish over and stir in:

24 small hard-shell clams, well scrubbed

3 medium leeks (white and tender green parts), cleaned thoroughly and cut crosswise into 5mm (¼ in) slices

1 tsp chopped fresh thyme

¼ tsp saffron threads

Pinch of crushed chilli flakes

375ml (12floz) dry white wine

Cover the pan, reduce the heat to medium, and cook until the clams are completely open, 8 to 15 minutes. Discard any that do not open. Remove from the heat and remove the clams from the pan.

Shell the clams and return them to the pan. If leaving clams in the shell, add them. Add:

250ml (8floz) *Garlic Mayonnaise (Aïoli)*, 118, using the larger amount of garlic

Gently shake the frying pan and stir the sauce with a wooden spoon until it is thickened and coats the fish and clams. Stir in:

1 tsp fresh lemon juice

Season with:

Ground black pepper to taste

Ladle into warmed shallow bowls and sprinkle with:

1 tbsp chopped fresh parsley

Pass separately to float atop the soup:

Garlic croutons

Louisiana Court Bouillon

About 1.75 litres (2¾ pints)

A court bouillon is a light-flavoured broth used for cooking food, primarily fish, but also vegetables and meat. This is not a classic court bouillon but a spicy Cajun fish and tomato stew. Redfish or snapper is often used in this dish, but you can use any white flaky fish. We have added prawns, but feel free to omit or to add your favourite shellfish.

Heat in a large frying pan over medium heat:

3 tbsp vegetable oil

Add and cook, stirring, until lightly browned, about 5 minutes:

3 tbsp plain flour

Add and cook, stirring, just until softened, about 3 minutes:

90g (3oz) diced green peppers
60g (2oz) diced celery
60g (2oz) diced onions
2 cloves garlic, finely chopped
½ tsp dried thyme

Stir in:

Two 400g (14oz) tins whole plum tomatoes, drained and coarsely chopped
500ml (16floz) *Fish Stock, 21, Fish Fumet, 21, or Express Fish Broth, 28*

Bring to a boil, reduce the heat to medium-low, and simmer for 10 minutes. Stir in:

500g (1lb) flaky white fish fillets (such as haddock or snapper), cut into 5cm (2in) pieces
12 small prawns (about 125g/4oz), peeled and deveined

Cover and cook until the fish is opaque in the centre, about 3 minutes. Season with:

2 tsp Worcestershire sauce
1 tsp salt
¾ - 1¼ tsp Tabasco sauce

Stir in:

125-185g (4-6oz) cooked long-grain rice

Taste and adjust the seasonings, adding more Worcestershire and Tabasco sauce as desired. Ladle into warmed bowls.

Charleston Crab Soup

About 1 litre (1½ pints)

Whole crabs are sold in supermarkets. They are a nuisance to clean and pick yourself; the yield is somewhere between 10 and 15 percent (you would have to pick 7 to 10 crabs to obtain 500g/1lb of meat) and, unless you are highly skilled, each crab will take you about 10 minutes to clean. So if you want meat for recipes, buy prepicked, fresh – not pasteurized – lump crabmeat. This elegant soup is called she-crab soup when made with female crabs and their roe.

Melt in a large saucepan, over low heat:

45g (1½oz) unsalted butter

Whisk in:

3 tbsp plain flour

Cook, whisking, until the flour smells toasted but is not browned, about 3 minutes. Gradually whisk in:

750ml (24floz) milk
1 tsp Worcestershire sauce
¾ tsp Tabasco sauce

Bring to a boil, whisking, reduce the heat and simmer for about 5 minutes. Reduce the heat to low and stir in:

500g (1lb) lump crabmeat, picked over for shells and cartilage, with roe if available
1-2 tbsp dry sherry
¾ tsp salt

Taste and adjust the seasonings, adding more Tabasco sauce if desired. Heat gently just until the crab is warmed through. Ladle into warmed bowls. Garnish with:

Thinly sliced spring onion greens

HANDLING FISH AT HOME

Refrigerators are not cold enough to store fish, which keeps almost twice as well at 0° or 0.5°C (32° or 33°F) as it does at 4.5°C (40°F), the temperature of most refrigerators. Fill the vegetable bin or a baking tin with ice (or ice packs) and bury your wrapped fish in there. Although some fish will retain their quality for as long as ten days, many of those days are spent in getting the fish from the water to your home. Even a farm-raised fish is probably at least three days old by the time it reaches your supermarket. So it makes sense to buy fish the day you are going to eat it, or at most the day before.

Caribbean Callaloo

About 3 litres (5 pints)

Callaloo is the name given to a family of plants favoured in the Caribbean for their tart green leaves. Callaloo leaves are occasionally found tinned in Caribbean markets, but fresh spinach and Swiss chard are good substitutes. Tinned callaloo leaves cook more quickly than fresh. The soup includes okra, which should not be cooked in an aluminium, iron or unlined copper pot. This soup can also be served over rice as a hearty main course.

Place in a soup pot and cook, stirring, over medium heat until almost crisp:

3 slices bacon, thinly sliced crosswise

Leaving the bacon in the pot, pour off all but 1 tsp of the fat and add:

250g (8oz) ham, cubed
1 medium onion, chopped
1 clove garlic, finely chopped
3 spring onions, thinly sliced

Cook, stirring, until the onions are tender but not browned, 5 to 10 minutes.

Stir in:

500g (1lb) callaloo, spinach or Swiss chard, trimmed, washed, dried and coarsely chopped
2.5 litres (4 pints) *Chicken Stock*, 22
¼ tsp dried thyme

Cover, bring to a boil and simmer for 5 minutes. Reduce the heat, remove the cover and add:

250g (8oz) lump crabmeat, picked over for shells and cartilage, or sliced raw prawns
250g (8oz) white fish fillets (such as cod, halibut or sea bass), cooked or raw
½ tsp salt
250g (8oz) fresh okra, sliced, or frozen sliced okra
250ml (8floz) unsweetened coconut milk
Ground black pepper to taste

Simmer until the okra and fish are cooked, about 10 minutes. The fillets will break up as they cook. Serve immediately.

Thai Clam Pot

4 to 6 servings

Have ready:

8 cloves garlic, thinly slivered

8 spring onions, cut into 5cm (2in) lengths, then lengthwise in half

1 tsp crushed chilli flakes

250ml (8floz) rice wine mixed with 250ml (8floz) water

1.5kg (3lb) small hard-shell clams, well washed and drained

30g (1oz) fresh basil leaves, cut into thin strips

2 tbsp fish sauce

When ready to cook, bring to a rolling boil in a large pot:

3-4 litres (5-6½ pints) water

Add and cook until done, 2 to 3 minutes:

125g (4oz) thin somen noodles or angel-hair pasta

Drain immediately in a sieve and rinse lightly to remove starch. While the noodles are cooking, heat a heavy pot large enough to hold the clams over high heat until hot. Add:

2 tbsp peanut oil

Heat, swirling, until very hot but not smoking. Add the garlic, spring onions and crushed chilli flakes. Stir for about 15 seconds. Standing back, add the wine mixture, cover and bring to a boil. Add the clams, cover and return the liquid to a boil. Immediately reduce the heat to medium and cook until the clams have just opened, 7 to 8 minutes, shaking the pot 3 or 4 times to ensure that the clams cook evenly.

Add the basil and stir it thoroughly into the liquid. Cover and cook for 30 to 45 seconds. Add the fish sauce and stir thoroughly. Divide the noodles among individual bowls, add the clams and pour the broth over them. Serve immediately.

Sardinian Seafood Stew (Cassola)

4 to 6 servings

Soak in a small amount of hot water to cover for 30 minutes:

5 sun-dried tomato halves, preferably packed in oil

Drain and reserve the soaking liquid. Chop the tomatoes and reserve. Scrub individually with a vegetable brush:

500g (1lb) small mussels

Remove the beards. Discard any damaged mussels or those that do not close with a sharp tap on the counter. Place the mussels in a large soup pot, along with:

250ml (8floz) dry white wine

Cover the pot, place it over high heat, and cook, shaking the pot occasionally, until most of the mussels are opened, about 10 minutes. Discard any mussels that have not opened. Lift the mussels from the pot and remove most of them from their shells, but reserve a few in the shells for garnish. Continue to cook the cooking liquid until reduced to about 250ml (8floz) Pour through a sieve lined with several layers of dampened muslin or paper towels, and set aside. Place in a large saucepan along with the drained sun-dried tomatoes:

1 tbsp olive oil
1 medium onion, chopped
15g (½ oz) chopped fresh basil

Cook, stirring, over medium heat until the onions are golden, 10 to 15 minutes. Add:

250g (8oz) squid, cleaned and cut into bite-sized pieces

Increase the heat to high and cook, stirring almost constantly, until the squid begins to brown, 3 to 4 minutes. Add the reserved tomato soaking liquid along with:

1 tsp finely chopped garlic
1 dried red chilli pepper

Cook, stirring, until the liquid is evaporated, about 2 minutes. Stir in the reserved mussel cooking liquid along with:

560g (18oz) chopped, seeded, peeled tomatoes, fresh or tinned

500ml (16floz) *Fish Stock, 21, Fish Fumet, 21, Express Fish Broth, 28,* **or water**

Bring to a boil, reduce the heat to medium-low, and simmer, stirring occasionally, until the squid is tender, about 1 hour. Remove the chilli pepper and stir in:

2 tbsp red wine vinegar

Add:

500g (1lb) prawns, peeled, deveined, if desired
500g (1lb) firm white-fleshed fish fillets or steaks, such as snapper, halibut or monkfish

Cover and cook until the fish is tender, 5 to 10 minutes. The fish fillets will break up as they cook. Add the shelled mussels to the pot and cook just until heated through. Season with:

Salt and ground black pepper

Garnish with the reserved mussels in their shells and sprinkle with:

Chopped fresh parsley

Serve with:

Crusty French bread

Lobster Bisque

About 2 litres (3¼ pints)

A classic lobster bisque derives its deep flavour and dusky-pink colour from beef stock and its distinctive, velvety body from rice. The soup should be thick but not too thick, so thin it as necessary before serving.

Combine in a wide, deep pot or flameproof casserole and bring to a boil over high heat:

1.25 litres (2 pints) water
500ml (16floz) dry white wine
500ml (16floz) Fish Stock, 21, or Fish Fumet, 21
250ml (8floz) Classic Beef Stock, 24, or Brown Beef Stock, 24

Place in the pot back side down:

2 live lobsters (625-750g/ 1¼ -1½ lb each)

Cover the pot tightly, return the liquid to a boil and cook for 6 minutes. Turn the lobsters with tongs, cover the pot and cook for 6 minutes more. Remove from the heat. Remove the lobsters from the broth. When cool enough to handle, remove the meat from the shells and discard the coral and green matter (tomalley). Cover and refrigerate the meat. Chop the shells and bodies, return to the broth, and simmer, uncovered, for 45 minutes. Strain through a fine-mesh sieve and discard the solids. You need 1.5 litres (2½ pints) of broth. If you have more, boil it over high heat until reduced to 1.5 litres (2½ pints). If you have less, add water to make 1.5 litres (2½ pints). Melt in a large saucepan over medium heat:

45-60g (1½-2oz) unsalted butter

Add and cook, stirring, until tender but not browned, 5 to 10 minutes:

125g (4oz) finely chopped onions
75g (2½ oz) finely chopped carrots
75g (2½ oz) finely chopped celery

Stir in the 1.5 litres (2½ pints) of broth along with:

280g (9oz) chopped, seeded, peeled tomatoes, fresh or tinned
60g (2oz) long-grain rice
1 bay leaf
1½ tsp chopped fresh tarragon, or ½ tsp dried
1 tsp sweet or hot paprika
½ tsp finely chopped garlic
½ tsp salt
¼ tsp dried thyme
⅛ tsp cayenne pepper

Bring to a boil, reduce the heat and simmer, partially covered, for 40 minutes. Meanwhile, cut the lobster meat into 5mm (¼ in) dice. Melt in a medium frying pan over medium heat:

30-60g (1-2oz) unsalted butter

Add the lobster meat and cook, stirring, until heated through. Stir in:

60ml (2floz) Cognac or brandy
¼ tsp salt
¼ tsp ground white pepper, preferably freshly ground

Cook, stirring, until nearly all of the liquid is evaporated. Set aside 5 tbsp of the meat for garnish. Add the rest of the meat and any juices to the soup mixture. Remove the bay leaf. In a food processor or, preferably, a blender, purée the soup in small batches until smooth. Return the soup to the saucepan and stir in the reserved lobster meat along with:

125-250ml (4-8floz) double cream

Heat the bisque through over low heat. Thin, if necessary, with:

Fish stock or milk

Remove from the heat and season with:

Drops of fresh lemon juice to taste
Salt and ground white pepper
Cayenne pepper

If you wish, garnish each serving with:

2 tbsp chopped fresh tarragon or parsley

LOBSTERS

Lobsters fall neatly into two groups: those with claws and those without. Those with claws – in the US commonly called Northern (Maine) lobster even when taken from Canada or elsewhere on the North Atlantic coast – are generally agreed to be superior and are, in fact, true lobsters. Those without, which have excellent tail meat, most often are seen in the form of frozen lobster tails. European lobsters are very similar to Northern lobster. There are also European spiny lobsters; these are eaten locally. All lobsters can be used interchangeably in recipes, although those without claws obviously have less meat than those with claws.

PRAWN BISQUE

This bisque is a delightful treat. Prepare *Lobster Bisque, opposite,* substituting 500g (1lb) shell-on prawns for the lobsters. Steam the prawns until the shells turn pink and curl, about 2 minutes, and simmer the shells for only 30 minutes.

ABOUT
MEAT AND
POULTRY
SOUPS & STEWS

*M*any of these robust soups and stews can be served as a full meal. All the meat soups here require long simmering. This allows economical cuts of meat to become tender and impart their full flavour to the soup or stew.

Tough but flavourful stewing hens are difficult to find, so the poultry soups and stews in this section are made with chicken. Because chicken cooks fast, it is easy to prepare substantial soup or stew quickly. All chicken, especially white meat, becomes dry and stringy with overcooking. So reheat the soup or stew gently, just until hot. Improvise your own versions with seasonal ingredients on hand.

Chicken Gumbo, 99

Beef Stew

6 to 8 servings

Pat dry:

1kg (2lb) boneless stewing beef, such as chuck, cut into 5cm (2in) cubes

Season the meat with:

½ -1 tsp dried herbs (thyme, marjoram, savoury, oregano and/or basil)

½ tsp salt

½ tsp ground black pepper

Dredge the meat with:

75g (2½ oz) plain flour

Shake off any excess flour. Heat in a flameproof casserole over medium-high heat:

2 tbsp olive or vegetable oil, bacon fat, beef drippings or other fat

Add the meat in batches and brown on all sides, being careful not to crowd the pan or scorch the meat. Remove with a slotted spoon. Pour off all but 2 tbsp of fat from the pan (add more if needed). Add:

60g (2oz) chopped onions

45g (1½ oz) chopped carrots

30g (1oz) chopped celery

30g (1oz) chopped leeks (optional)

2 tbsp chopped garlic (optional)

Cover and cook, stirring often, over medium heat until the onions are softened, about 5 minutes. Add:

2 bay leaves

½ -1 tsp of the same herbs used to season the meat

½ tsp salt

½ tsp ground black pepper

Add enough to cover the meat at least halfway:

500-750ml (16-24floz) *Beef Stock*, 24, or *Chicken Stock*, 22, dry red or white wine, or beer

Bring to a boil. Reduce the heat, cover, and simmer over low heat

until the meat is fork-tender, 1½ to 2 hours. Add:

2-3 carrots, peeled and cut into 2.5cm (1in) chunks

3 or 4 boiling potatoes, peeled and cut into 2.5cm (1in) chunks

2 turnips, peeled and cut into 2.5cm (1in) chunks

2 parsnips, peeled and cut into 2.5cm (1in) chunks

Cover and cook until the vegetables are tender, 35 to 40 minutes.

Remove the pan from the heat and skim off any fat from the surface. Taste and adjust the seasonings. If you wish, thicken the sauce by stirring together and whisking into the stew:

1-1½ tbsp *Kneaded Butter*, below

Simmer, stirring, until thickened. Garnish with:

Chopped fresh parsley

Kneaded Butter

About 2 tablespoons

Known as beurre manié in French, kneaded butter is a convenient last-minute thickener, added to a cooked liquid just before serving. Kneaded butter is simply softened butter mixed with an equal proportion of flour and kneaded by hand or with a fork. It is shaped into balls the size of a pea that can be whisked into a simmering liquid. Once you have

added the butter, bring the liquid back to a simmer and remove the pan from the heat; extended cooking or boiling may cause the liquid to separate. Since the flour is not cooked, it can leave a raw flour taste, so use kneaded butter sparingly. Knead together by hand or with a fork:

15g (½ oz) softened butter

1 tbsp flour

Borscht

About 2 litres (3¼ pints)

This is the original Russian borscht, meaty and brimming with tomatoes and cabbage. The beetroots are roasted instead of boiled, for added flavour.

Preheat the oven to 200°C (400°F) Gas 6. Scrub:

375g (12oz) beetroot

Wrap the beetroots together in aluminium foil and roast on a baking tray until they can easily be pierced with a fork, about 1 hour. Let cool, peel, then slice and cut into thin strips. While the beets are roasting, prepare:

500g (1lb) boneless beef chuck, cubed, or 750g (1½ lb) pork spareribs, cut into single ribs

Lightly dredge with:

Plain flour

Heat in a soup pot, over medium-high heat:

2 tbsp vegetable oil

Add the meat and brown on all sides. Stir in:

Just over 1 litre (1½ pints) *Brown Beef Stock*, 24, or water
Two 400g (14oz) tins whole plum tomatoes, drained and chopped

Bring to a boil, reduce the heat and simmer, partially covered, until the meat is almost tender, about 30 minutes. Stir in:

180g (6oz) shredded green or red cabbage
1 medium onion, chopped
2 medium carrots, peeled and sliced
2 medium celery stalks, sliced

1½ tsp tomato purée

Simmer, partially covered, until the vegetables and meat are tender, about 30 minutes. Stir in the beetroot along with:

2 tbsp red wine vinegar
2 tsp fresh lemon juice
2 cloves garlic, finely chopped
½ tsp salt, or to taste
¾ tsp ground black pepper
1½ tsp sugar (optional)

Simmer, partially covered, for 15 minutes. Thin the soup with water if necessary. Ladle into warmed bowls. Garnish with:

Sour cream
Snipped fresh dill

Scotch Broth

About 1.5 litres (2½ pints)

Funny how barley, a crop traced back to 7000 B.C., continues to surprise and delight today, as if every dish it appears in reinvents its roast-nut taste. The off-white oval kernels most commonly sold as pearl barley have had the tough husk, bran and germ ground away, yielding the endosperm, a kernel that cooks much faster than hulled, or whole, barley. This Scottish classic is hundreds of years old in origin and is known for its use of barley and lamb.

Bring to a boil in a soup pot:

1.5 litres (2½ pints) water
750g (1½ lb) lamb shoulder, trimmed of fat and cut into 1cm (½ in) pieces

Reduce the heat, and simmer for 10 minutes. Skim the impurities from the surface. Stir in:

100g (3½ oz) pearl barley
3 medium leeks (white part only), cleaned thoroughly and chopped
1 large carrot, peeled and diced
1 large celery stalk, diced
½ tsp salt

Bring to a boil, reduce the heat and simmer, partially covered, until the meat is tender, about 1½ hours. Replenish the water as needed. Spoon off the fat from the surface and season with:

Salt and ground black pepper to taste
2 tbsp chopped fresh parsley

Pennsylvania Dutch Chicken Sweetcorn Soup

About 1.5 litres (2½ pints)

Use any type of wide egg noodle you like in this chicken sweetcorn soup. Some recipes call for a garnish of popcorn to reinforce the sweetcorn flavour and to add some crunch to the soup.

Bring to a boil in a soup pot:

1.5 litres (2½ pints) water, or 750ml (24floz) water and 750ml (24floz) Chicken Stock, 22

750g-1kg(1½ -2lb) chicken parts, or ½ whole chicken, cut into serving pieces

1 tsp salt (½ tsp if using chicken stock)

⅛ tsp ground black pepper

Skim the impurities from the surface. Reduce the heat and simmer, covered, until the chicken is well cooked, about 1 hour. Remove the chicken, discard the skin and bones, shred the meat and set aside. (At this point you can remove the surface fat with a small ladle.) Bring the stock to a boil. Stir in:

180g (6oz) short, wide egg noodles

180g (6oz) fresh or frozen sweetcorn kernels

Cook, stirring occasionally, until the noodles are tender but firm. Stir in the shredded chicken along with:

1 hard-boiled egg, chopped

1½ tbsp chopped fresh parsley

Ladle into warmed bowls.

Chicken Gumbo

About 2.5 litres (4 pints)

Quingombo, *an African Congo word for okra, became "gumbo" in Louisiana and came to be known as a thick soup/stew thickened either with okra or with filé powder (ground sassafras root). This version of chicken gumbo gets its distinctive taste from a wonderful dark roux of oil and flour and a mix of dried spices. Make this recipe a day or two ahead if you can, for it only improves with time.*

Combine in a small bowl and reserve:

60g (2oz) chopped celery
60g (2oz) chopped onions
125g (4oz) chopped green peppers

Combine in a large plastic or paper bag:

2 tsp cayenne pepper
1½ tsp salt
1 tsp ground black pepper
1 tsp garlic powder

Add and shake until completely covered:

1 whole chicken (about 1.5kg/ 3lb), cut into serving pieces

Add and shake again:

75g (2½ oz) plain flour

Heat in a large cast-iron or other frying pan over medium heat:

2-4 tbsp vegetable oil

Add and brown the chicken pieces on all sides, 5 to 10 minutes. Remove and set aside. Add to the pan, scraping up the browned bits:

125ml (4floz) vegetable oil

Whisk in:

75g (2½ oz) plain flour

Cook, stirring often, over medium-low heat until the roux turns reddish brown, 5 to 6 minutes. Gently stir with a long-handled wooden spoon, using caution, because the roux is extremely hot and sticks to the skin. (If black specks appear, the roux is burned – so begin again in a clean pot.) Remove from the heat, add the reserved vegetables, and stir until the roux stops bubbling, 1 to 2 minutes. Carefully add the roux and vegetable mixture to a soup pot.

Whisk in:

2 litres (3¼ pints) Chicken Stock, 22, or Brown Chicken Stock, 22

Bring to a boil, whisking. Reduce the heat and add the chicken. Simmer until the chicken is cooked through, about 30 to 45 minutes. Remove the chicken from the pot and discard the skin and bones, shred the meat and reserve. Stir into the soup pot:

375g (12oz) andouille or chorizo sausage, cut into thin slices or small cubes
1 tbsp chopped garlic

Simmer until the sausage is cooked through, about 10 minutes. Stir in the reserved chicken meat along with:

90g (3oz) chopped spring onions
Salt to taste
Tabasco sauce to taste

Ladle into warmed bowls. Garnish with:

Sliced spring onion greens

Puerto Rican Chicken Rice Soup (Asopao de Pollo)

About 2.25 litres (3½ pints)

This dish is traditionally made with annatto seeds, which give the soup its characteristically yellow colour; this recipe uses ground annatto, but it can be omitted. Serve this soup/stew as soon as it cooks, before the rice absorbs the broth.

Combine:

1½ tsp garlic powder
1½ tsp onion powder
1½ tsp dried oregano
¾ tsp salt
¾ tsp ground black pepper

Rub the spice mixture, known as adobo seasoning, into the skin of:

1 whole chicken (about 1.5kg/ 3lb), cut into serving pieces

Heat in a soup pot, over medium-low heat:

3 tbsp vegetable oil

Add and cook, stirring, until tender but not browned, 5 to 10 minutes:

1 medium onion, diced
1 medium green pepper, diced
60g (2oz) diced ham
1 Scotch bonnet chilli pepper or 2 fresh jalapeño chilli peppers, seeded and diced
2 cloves garlic, finely chopped

Stir in the chicken along with:

1.5 litres (2½ pints) water
400g (14oz) tin diced tomatoes, drained
2 tsp ground annatto seeds (optional)

Bring to a boil, reduce the heat and simmer, partially covered, for 25 minutes. Stir in:

100g (3½oz) long-grain rice

Continue to simmer until the chicken and rice are cooked, about 20 minutes. Remove the chicken, discard the skin and bones and shred the meat. Return it to the soup and stir in:

155g (5oz) fresh or frozen peas
15g (½oz) chopped fresh coriander
60g (2oz) pimiento strips or sliced green olives stuffed with pimientos
Salt to taste

Simmer gently until the peas are just cooked through, 2 to 3 minutes. Ladle into warmed bowls.

Thai Chicken and Coconut Soup

About 1.5 litres (2½ pints)

Coconut milk is an infusion of grated coconut and boiling water or milk and is easily made from scratch. Pour 250ml (8floz) boiling water or milk over 100g (3½oz) fresh coconut shreds. Stir well, cover, and let steep for 30 minutes. Process the mixture (no more than 750ml/24floz at a time) in a blender or food processor for 1 minute. Pour all the shreds and milk into a damp clean cloth and press the liquid into a bowl, squeezing until the shreds are dry. The first pressing is referred to as thick coconut milk, and the yield is about 250ml (8floz). Cover, refrigerate and use within 3 days. Simmer kaffir lime leaves or lemon grass in the coconut milk first for a delicate citrus flavour.

Bring to a boil in a soup pot:

750ml (24floz) Chicken Stock, 22
660ml (21floz) unsweetened coconut milk

Reduce the heat and stir in:

2 small Thai chilli peppers or 3 fresh jalapeño chilli peppers, seeded and sliced
3 tbsp Thai fish sauce (nam pla) or soy sauce
1 tsp chopped peeled fresh ginger
⅛ tsp salt

Simmer for 10 minutes, then stir in:

500g (1lb) boneless, skinless chicken breasts, thinly sliced
2 tbsp fresh lime juice

Simmer, stirring occasionally, until the chicken is no longer pink, about 5 minutes. Ladle into warmed bowls. Garnish with:

Chopped fresh coriander

FISH SAUCE

Called nu'o'c ma'm in Vietnam and nam pla in Thailand, fish sauce is made by packing fish, usually anchovies, in crocks or barrels, covering them with brine and allowing them to ferment in the tropical sun over a period of months. The resulting brown liquid is drained off and used. The first siphoning is most highly prized and is usually reserved for dipping sauces. Fish sauce keeps indefinitely on the shelf.

Chicken Soup Cockaigne

About 2.5 litres (4 pints)

This soup has a few surprises. The sweet taste of parsnips adds a wonderful note, as does the ground mace. Vary the vegetables and substitute 4 tbsp rice or 60g (2oz) egg noodles for the potatoes, if desired.

Bring to a boil in a soup pot:

2 litres (3¼ pints) Chicken Stock, 22

1 whole chicken (about 1.5kg/ 3lb), cut into serving pieces, or 1.5kg (3lb) chicken parts

3 large carrots, diced

3 parsnips or 2 small purple-top turnips, peeled and diced (optional)

3 large celery stalks, diced

3 medium onions, coarsely chopped

2 medium leeks (white part only), cleaned thoroughly and sliced

2 large garlic cloves, finely chopped

1 Bouquet Garni, 17

¼ tsp ground black pepper

¼ tsp ground mace (optional)

Reduce the heat and simmer until the chicken is well cooked, about 1 hour. Remove the chicken to a plate and let cool. Meanwhile, add to the soup pot:

2 medium new potatoes, diced

Simmer until tender, 15 to 20 minutes. Discard the bouquet garni and turn off the heat. When the chicken is cool enough to handle, remove and discard the skin and bones. Shred the meat and add to the soup. Reheat over medium heat and season with:

4 tbsp chopped fresh parsley

Salt and ground black pepper to taste

Ladle into warmed bowls.

Vietnamese Beef Noodle Soup (Pho Bo)

4 to 6 servings

In Vietnam, this light, flavourful, visually exciting soup is a favourite for breakfast, lunch, and dinner. It has given rise to numerous pho restaurants all over Europe and the USA.

BEFORE COOKING:

Have ready:

4 tbsp thinly sliced peeled fresh ginger

1 medium onion, sliced

1.75kg (3½ lb) oxtail, cut into 5cm (2in) pieces (ask your butcher to do this)

7.5cm (3in) cinnamon stick

6 star anise

1 tbsp salt

1 tsp light or dark soy sauce

2.5cm (1in) piece Chinese yellow rock sugar (optional)

Place on a plate:

375g (12oz) round steak, sliced as thinly as possible (more easily done if partially frozen)

Place on a second plate:

2 serrano peppers, thinly sliced

24 fresh basil leaves, halved

60g (2oz) 5cm (2in) pieces spring onion, halved lengthwise

Place on a third plate:

140g (4½oz) bean sprouts

3 tbsp coarsely chopped fresh basil

Lime wedges

3 fresh chilli peppers, coarsely chopped

TO COOK:

Heat a large soup pot over medium-high heat. When fairly hot, turn in the ginger and onion slices. Cook, stirring, until fragrant. Add the oxtail and cook, stirring, briefly. Stir in:

3.5 litres (6 pints) cold water

Bring to a boil. Skim off the impurities that rise to the surface. Stir in the cinnamon, star anise, salt, soy sauce and rock sugar if using. Reduce the heat and simmer the soup for 2½ to 3 hours, skimming as needed. Strain and reserve. About 30 minutes before the broth is done, soak in cold water to cover:

375g (12oz) dried flat rice stick noodles (*banh pho*)

Bring to a boil in a large pot:

4 litres (6½ pints) water

Add the rice stick noodles. Cook for about 1 minute. Drain.

TO SERVE:

Divide the noodles among individual soup bowls. Add the slices of raw beef to each bowl, arranging them attractively. Divide the serrano peppers, basil leaves and spring onions among the bowls. While arranging the individual soup bowls, bring the beef broth to a boil over high heat. Immediately fill each bowl with the boiling broth and serve. If the broth is added at the table, diners have the pleasure of watching it cook the beef and noodles. Place the plate of bean sprouts, basil, lime and chilli peppers on the table, allowing diners to help themselves.

RICE STICK NOODLES

These thin, flat, translucent rice noodles should be soaked for 30 minutes in cold water, then boiled for 4 to 7 minutes before being added to any dish. They are most commonly used in pad thai and other stir-fried dishes and soups. Rice sticks are known as *banh pho* in Vietnam and *jantabon* in Thailand. Asian noodles are best understood by the type of flour or starch with which they are made. When looking for substitutes, choose noodles in the same starch family.

Oxtail Soup

About 1.25 litres (2 pints)

One story claims this rich meaty soup was born of necessity during the French Reign of Terror in 1793. Historically, hides were delivered to the tanneries complete with tails. These were commonly thrown away, until one day a hungry nobleman pleaded for a tail and made it into soup.

Heat in a soup pot over medium-high heat:

1½ tbsp extra-virgin olive oil

Add and brown on all sides:

1kg (2lb) oxtail (about 1 disjointed oxtail)

Stir in:

1.5 litres (2½ pints) water
1 large carrot, peeled and diced
1 large celery stalk, diced
1 large onion, diced

2 cloves garlic, peeled
4 black peppercorns

Bring to a boil, reduce the heat and simmer, partially covered, until the meat comes effortlessly from the bone, 3 to 4 hours. As the water evaporates during cooking, add only enough water to keep the meat submerged. Remove the oxtail from the soup. Discard the fat and bones and reserve the meat. Refrigerate the soup until cold, then remove the fat. When ready to serve, return the meat to the soup. Heat and season with:

¼ tsp salt

Ladle into warmed bowls. Garnish with:

Chopped fresh parsley

Pass at the table:

Ground black pepper

OXTAIL SOUP WITH VEGETABLES

The rich flavour of oxtail goes well with the tender vegetables in this soup. Prepare Oxtail Soup, left, adding with the salt: 1 medium leek (white part only), cut into thin strips; 1 small carrot, cut into thin strips; 1 small celery stalk, cut into thin strips; ¼ tsp additional salt. Simmer until the vegetables are tender, about 15 minutes. Add the meat and complete as directed.

French Simmered Beef and Vegetables (Pot-au-Feu)

About 2.5 litres (4 pints); 4 to 6 servings

This hearty French boiled dinner features a variety of meats, mostly beef, and vegetables. The cooking broth is strained, seasoned and served first in warmed bowls, then the meat and marrowbones are presented on a serving platter, accompanied by mustard and cornichons, and toast on which to spread the succulent marrow.

Combine in a large soup pot, and cover with cold water:

1.25kg (2½ lb) beef rib joints, cut into pieces
4 beef marrowbones, wrapped in muslin
1kg (2lb) beef shin, cut into 5cm (2in) thick slices

Bring to a boil, reduce the heat to low and simmer, partially covered, for 2 hours. Stir in:

4 chicken thighs, skin removed
375g (12oz) whole sausage
4 medium carrots, cut into 2.5cm (1in) pieces
4 medium leeks (white and tender green parts), cleaned thoroughly, halved lengthwise and cut into 2.5cm (1in) pieces
2 medium turnips, peeled and cut into 2.5cm (1in) pieces
3 medium celery stalks, cut into 2.5cm (1in) pieces

Simmer, partially covered, until the chicken is cooked, 30 to 40 minutes. Remove and reserve the meat and vegetables. Strain the broth and return it to the pot. Reduce to 2.5 litres (4 pints) over high heat. Slice the beef shin and sausage, then arrange the meat, vegetables and marrowbones on a platter. Cover with foil and keep warm in a very low oven. Skim the fat off the surface of the broth with a ladle.

Season with:

1½ tsp salt
Ground black pepper to taste

Heat the broth and ladle into warmed bowls. Serve the meat platter accompanied with:

Dijon or whole-grain mustard
Coarse salt
Cornichons
Toasted sliced French bread

Irish Stew

4 to 6 servings

The potatoes in this recipe are cut in two different ways because they serve different purposes. Those that are sliced break down during the long cooking and thicken the stew without the addition of flour. The halved potatoes cook to tender and add soft bite to the stew.

Preheat the oven to 165°C (325°F) Gas 3.

Heat in a flameproof casserole over medium heat:

2 tbsp vegetable oil or 30g (1oz) unsalted butter

Add and cook without browning, until softened:

2 medium onions, chopped

Stir in:

1.5kg (3lb) boneless lamb stew meat, cut into 2.5cm (1in) cubes, or 1.5kg (3lb) lamb shoulder chops

2 tsp fresh thyme leaves, or ¾ tsp dried

Salt and ground black pepper to taste

Mix in:

2 medium boiling potatoes, peeled and sliced

750ml (24floz) Chicken Stock, 22, or water

½ tsp Worcestershire sauce

Add:

4 medium potatoes, peeled and halved

Cover tightly and bake for 1 hour. Remove from the oven and add, stirring:

8 medium carrots, peeled and cut diagonally into 1cm (½ in) slices

4 tbsp pearl barley

60ml (2floz) double cream

Cover and return to the oven. Bake until the meat is fork-tender and barley is softened, 45 to 60 minutes more.

Season with:

Salt and ground black pepper

Serve sprinkled with:

Chopped fresh parsley

Mulligatawny Soup

About 1.25 litres (2 pints)

The predecessors of this version were created by local cooks in southern India. The countless variations are all curried and then smoothed with coconut milk or cream.

Skin, bone and cut into bite-sized pieces:

1kg (2lb) chicken thighs

Heat over medium-high heat in a soup pot:

3 tbsp vegetable oil

Add and cook, stirring, until golden brown, 7 to 8 minutes:

1 medium onion, thinly sliced

Add and cook, stirring, for 30 seconds:

2 cloves garlic, finely chopped
2.5cm (1in) piece fresh ginger, peeled and finely chopped
1 tbsp curry powder

Add the chicken along with:

2 tbsp water

Cook, stirring, until the chicken loses its raw colour and the oil sizzles and pools around the meat, 3 to 4 minutes.

Stir in:

1 litre (1½ pints) Chicken Stock, 22
½ tsp salt

Bring to a boil, reduce the heat to medium and simmer until the chicken is cooked through, 20 to 30 minutes. Stir in:

250ml (8floz) unsweetened coconut milk (optional)

Simmer for 5 minutes more.

Divide among 4 bowls:

125g (4oz) hot cooked rice

Ladle the soup on top and garnish with:

Fresh coriander leaves
Lemon wedges
Chopped apples

Madras Curry Powder

About 125g (4oz)

Curry (or kari) leaves are the leaves of the kari plant, used to flavour the cooking of southern and southwestern India. Fresh leaves are sold at Indian grocers. You may substitute dried leaves, but their flavour is much less pungent.

Toast in a heated frying pan over medium heat until a shade darker and fragrant, about 4 minutes:

6 tbsp whole coriander seeds
4 tbsp whole cumin seeds
3 tbsp *chana dal* or yellow split peas
1 tbsp black peppercorns
1 tbsp black mustard seeds
5 dried red chilli peppers
10 fresh or dried curry leaves (optional)

Combine the toasted spices with:

2 tbsp fenugreek seeds

Grind the mixture to a powder in batches in a spice mill or electric coffee grinder. Mix well with:

3 tbsp turmeric

Store in an airtight container in a cool place.

Barley Soup with Sausages (Minestra d'Orzo)

About 4 litres (6½ pints)

This soup is inspired by the foods of Italy's mountainous Tyrol at Austria's border. On its native turf, it would be flavoured with "speck", meaty chunks of pork deeply smoked and cured with salt, juniper, garlic and spices. Smoked kielbasa or bratwurst can be substituted. Serve with thick slices of country bread.

Cook in a medium frying pan, or on a medium-hot outdoor barbecue or stovetop grill, until browned on all sides and heated through:

185g (6oz) deeply smoked sausages

Slice the sausages thinly and place in a large soup pot along with:

4 litres (6½ pints) *Vegetable Stock,* **20, or** *Chicken Stock,* **22**
250g (8oz) pearl barley
2 large bay leaves, crumbled

Bring to a boil, reduce the heat and simmer, partially covered, for 30 minutes. Meanwhile, heat in a large frying pan over medium heat:

2 tbsp extra-virgin olive oil

Add:

½ large head green cabbage, chopped

Cook, stirring, until the cabbage begins to colour, 5 to 10 minutes. Add:

2 medium onions, finely chopped
1 large carrot, peeled and finely chopped
1 large celery stalk with leaves, finely chopped
3 tbsp fresh parsley leaves, chopped
Two 7.5cm (3in) sprigs fresh rosemary, or 2 tsp dried

Cook, stirring often, until the onions are browned, 10 to 15 minutes. Stir in:

3 tbsp fresh marjoram leaves, chopped, or 1 tbsp dried
1 large clove garlic, finely chopped

Add 250ml (8floz) liquid from the soup pot and scrape the bottom of the pan to loosen any browned bits. Stir the contents of the pan into the soup pot along with:

2 red or white new potatoes, peeled and diced

Cover and simmer gently until the barley is tender but not mushy and the potatoes are cooked but firm, about 30 minutes more. If the soup is too thick, thin with water as needed. Season with:

2½ tsp salt
1 tsp ground black pepper

Ladle into warmed bowls. Sprinkle each serving with:

1-2 tbsp grated aged Montasio or provolone cheese

Beef Chilli (Chilli con Carne)

6 to 8 servings

For more flavour in this dish (opposite), make your own chilli powder. As a rule, use smaller amounts of hotter chillies, such as arbol or serrano, and larger amounts of the mild and midrange varieties, such as ancho, mild New Mexico (red Anaheim) and guajillo. The rice and sour cream help cool the heat of this dish. Bear in mind that any left-overs will become hotter from the heat of the chillies the longer they are kept.

Toast in a frying pan over medium heat for 1 to 2 minutes:

1 recipe *New Mexican Chilli Powder*, right, or 100g (3½ oz) chilli powder

Set aside. Pat dry:

1.5kg (3lb) beef chuck, trimmed and cut into 1cm (½ in) cubes

Season with:

1-2 tsp salt

Heat in a cast-iron frying pan over medium-high heat:

1 tbsp olive oil

Brown the meat in batches, adding more oil if needed. Remove the browned meat to a flameproof casserole.

Add to the cast-iron frying pan:

1 tbsp olive oil
2 large onions, finely chopped
10 cloves garlic, finely chopped
7 fresh jalapeño chillies, stemmed, seeded, and finely chopped
½ tsp salt

Cook, stirring often, over medium-high heat until the vegetables are softened, 6 to 8 minutes. Remove to the casserole with the meat. Stir the toasted spices into the meat mixture and cook for 2 minutes over medium-high heat. Add:

Two 400g (14oz) tins plum tomatoes, with juice
1 tbsp red wine vinegar
1.5 litres (2½ pints) water

Season with:

Salt to taste

Simmer, uncovered, until the meat is tender and the sauce is reduced and thickened, about 1½ hours.

Serve with:

Hot cooked rice
Sour cream

New Mexican Chilli Powder

About 50g (1¾ oz)

Based on ground dried chillies, this chilli powder is a blend created to flavour Southwestern dishes. It is as individual as the person who prepares it. Sometimes it is very dark, sometimes a rusty red. This chilli powder is best toasted before use. Stir it in a medium frying pan over the lowest heat until you can smell the spices.

Combine in a small bowl:

5 tbsp ground mild chilli peppers, such as New Mexico, pasilla or ancho
2 tbsp dried oregano
1½ tbsp ground cumin
½ tsp cayenne pepper, or to taste

Ohio Farmhouse Sausage Chilli

4 to 6 servings

A delicious "warmer-upper" after a fine tramp in the woods on a chilly day. Loose pork sausage meat is used instead of minced beef. Look for some that is not heavily spiced. Corn bread is perfect served alongside.

Brown in a large frying pan:

500g (1lb) pork sausage
1 large onion, chopped

Towards the end of the browning, add:

1 celery stalk, diced

When the celery is softened, add:

Two 400g (14oz) tins whole tomatoes, chopped
500ml (16floz) tomato juice or *Chicken Broth*, 29, or a mixture
1-2 tbsp maple syrup or molasses
2 tsp ground cumin
1½ tsp powdered sage
½ tsp ground black pepper

Simmer for 20 minutes. Add:

625g (1¼lb) cooked red kidney beans, drained and rinsed

Simmer for 15 minutes more.

Serve with:

Mature Cheddar cheese, cubed
Soft Corn Bread, 124

Brunswick Stew

6 to 8 servings

This Southern American speciality is commonly served as a side dish with barbecue but can easily stand on its own as a main course. Chicken, lima beans and sweetcorn are the main ingredients, with such meats as rabbit, pork or even squirrel sometimes added to the pot as well. This version includes barbecue sauce, which makes it especially rich and thick.

Rinse and pat dry:

2.5kg (5lb) chicken parts

Season with:

Salt and ground black pepper to taste

½ tsp cayenne pepper (optional)

Heat in a large, heavy flameproof casserole over medium-high heat until shimmery:

2 tbsp bacon fat or vegetable oil

Add the chicken pieces in small batches and brown on all sides; remove them to a plate as they are done. Remove all but 2 tbsp of the fat in the pan. Reduce the heat to medium and add:

125g (4oz) chopped onions

125g (4oz) chopped celery

Cook, stirring occasionally, until the vegetables are just tender, 5 to 7 minutes. Return the chicken with the accumulated juices to the pan. Add:

625g (1¼ lb) lima or green beans, fresh or frozen

440g (14oz) barbecued pork or smoked ham, cut into 1cm (½ in) chunks (optional)

280-375g (9-12oz) chopped seeded peeled tomatoes, fresh or tinned

250ml (8floz) barbecue sauce

250ml (8floz) tomato purée

250ml (8floz) *Chicken Stock*, 22, or water

1 tbsp finely chopped garlic (optional)

2 bay leaves

Salt and ground black pepper to taste

Cayenne pepper to taste

Bring the stew to a boil over high heat. Reduce the heat to low, cover the pan and simmer gently until the chicken is nearly tender, 35 to 45 minutes. Add:

560g (18oz) sweetcorn kernels, fresh or frozen

Simmer, uncovered, for 10 minutes more. Skim any fat from the gravy with a spoon. Season the stew to taste with:

Salt and ground black pepper

Several drops of Worcestershire sauce

Several drops of Tabasco sauce

If you wish, sprinkle the top with:

Chopped fresh parsley

Fresh breadcrumbs, toasted

MAKING BREADCRUMBS

Place slices of good, stale bread on a baking tray in a very low oven for 1 to 2 hours; do not let them brown. Grind the dry bread into crumbs with the grating blade of a food processor or a hand grater. Spread on a baking tray in a 190°C (375°F) Gas 5 oven for 10 to 15 minutes. For seasoned bread-crumbs, add ½ tsp salt to every 90g (3oz) dry breadcrumbs; melt 75g (2½oz) butter per 90g (3oz) crumbs in a frying pan and toss the crumbs in the butter until browned. Spices, herbs or grated cheese can be added while toasting the breadcrumbs. Cook until the crumbs are golden brown.

MacLeid's Rockcastle Chilli

8 to 10 servings

This is camping chef extraordinaire and good friend Matt MacLeid's Saturday-night staple on our camping trips to the Rockcastle River Gorge.

Sauté in a large frying pan until cracklings are golden brown:

250g (8oz) bacon, diced

Remove the bacon using a slotted spoon. In the drippings, sauté briefly:

750g (1½ lb) rump steak, coarsely minced or chopped in a food processor

6-12 large cloves garlic, coarsely chopped

2 large onions, coarsely chopped

Deglaze the frying pan until foam disappears, with:

375ml (12floz) bottle beer

Remove all to a large pot or flame-proof casserole. Stir in:

1kg (2lb) tinned tomatoes, with juice

400g (14oz) tin kidney beans, with juice

400g (14oz) tin cannellini beans, with juice

400g (14oz) tin pinto beans, with juice

6 tbsp ancho chilli powder

2 tbsp ground cumin

1 tbsp ground black pepper

375ml (12floz) water or one 375ml (12floz) bottle beer

Simmer for about 3 hours, covered, stirring occasionally to prevent sticking. Season to taste with:

Salt and ground black pepper

Tabasco sauce

Serve with:

***American Corn Bread*, 123**

Diced mature Cheddar cheese

MINCING MEAT

Now that the food processor is a fundamental tool in most kitchens, it is very easy to mince your own meat. By chopping your own meat, you have a better guarantee of freshness and fat content. The best cuts to use are chuck or shoulder. Trim away visible fat and cut the meat into 2.5cm (1in) cubes. Keep the meat thoroughly refrigerated before and after chopping. Place enough meat in the bowl of the processor to cover the blade by 2.5cm (1in), no more. Pulse the processor until the pieces of meat are uniformly small (about 2mm/ ⅛ in). Remove the chopped meat from the bowl and repeat the process until all the meat is done.

Cincinnati Chilli Cockaigne

6 servings

There are hundreds of so-called original recipes for John Kiradjieff's Cincinnati Chilli that he served for the first time in Cincinnati's first chilli parlour, The Empress. We particularly like this version of our hometown obsession, and we can guarantee without question that it is not the one of myth.

In a 4-6 litre (6½-10 pint) pot, bring to a boil:

1 litre (1½ pints) water

Add:

1kg (2lb) minced chuck

Stir until separated and reduce heat to a simmer. Add:

2 medium onions, finely chopped

5-6 cloves garlic, crushed

470g (15oz) tinned or bottled tomato sauce

2 tbsp cider vinegar

1 tbsp Worcestershire sauce

Stir and add:

10 peppercorns, ground

8 whole allspice, ground

8 whole cloves, ground

1 large bay leaf

2 tsp salt

2 tsp ground cinnamon

1½ tsp cayenne pepper

1 tsp ground cumin

15g (½ oz) unsweetened chocolate, grated

Return to a boil, then reduce the heat to a simmer, for 2½ hours cooking time in all. Cool uncovered and refrigerate overnight. Before serving, skim off all or most of the fat and discard. Reheat the chilli for a 2-Way, and serve over:

Cooked spaghetti

For a 3-Way, add:

Grated Cheddar cheese

For a 4-Way, sprinkle on:

Chopped onions

For a 5-Way, top each serving with:

4 tbsp cooked red kidney beans

Traditional side dishes also include:

Oyster crackers

Tabasco sauce

ABOUT **FRUIT** SOUPS

We include recipes for fruit soups that are traditionally served as first courses. Feel free to present them as desserts, however. Whichever place they occupy on your menu, they are easy to make, and they cleanse the palate. For fresh fruit, the best advice is to eat fruit that is local, in season and perfectly ripe.

Melon Soup, 115

Cherry Soup

About 1.5 litres (2½ pints)

We make this fruit soup in the summer with fresh cherries and serve it cold before the main course. In the winter, we use tinned or bottled cherries and serve it heated.

Have ready:

1kg (2lb) cherries, stemmed and stoned, or 500g (1lb) stemmed and stoned tinned cherries, drained

Place half of the cherries in a soup pot, along with:

500ml (16floz) water
500ml (16floz) Gewürztraminer or medium-dry white wine

Bring to a boil, reduce the heat and simmer until the cherries are soft, about 15 minutes. Purée until smooth. Stir together in a small bowl:

4 tbsp sugar
4 tsp cornflour

Add 3 tbsp of the cherry mixture to the cornflour and sugar and stir well. Return the cherry purée and the cherry paste to the pot and cook over high heat, whisking until thickened, about 5 minutes. Reduce the heat and stir in the reserved cherries along with:

1 tbsp fresh orange juice
1 tbsp fresh lemon juice
1 tsp grated orange zest

Simmer until warmed through. Taste for sweetness; if not sweet enough, add additional:

Sugar

If too sweet, add additional:

Lemon juice

Serve warm or cold, garnished with:

Dollop of sour cream or yoghurt
Fresh mint sprigs

CHERRIES

Stoned raw sweet cherries are incomparable in cold soups. The production of cherries has increased with the introduction of late-cropping black varieties. Look out for Stella, Merchant, Sasha, Hertford, Sunburst, Lapins and Colney from mid-June through to mid-July.

Sour cherries, another variety, are tastier after cooking, since they are very acid and heat helps them absorb sweetening. Although most commercial sour cherries are tinned, you may find fresh morellos, delightful with their red juice, or amarelles, with their clear juice, close to where they are grown. Sour cherries ripen a couple of weeks after sweet cherries. Montmorency, a morello, is a popular sour cherry, predominantly grown in the US, and is ideal for making jam. It is named after the town near Paris from which it originated.

All cherries are sent to market ripe. Choose them individually (never prepackaged) after tasting one for flavour. Select the largest, glossiest, plumpest and firmest with the greenest stems. For sweet cherries, choose the darkest; for sour cherries, the brightest. Avoid stemless cherries – the wound is an invitation to bacteria, as evidenced when there is brown around the stem scar. If there are soft or spoiling cherries in a bin, do not buy any. The taste of mould can permeate surrounding fruit.

To keep cherries, arrange them, without rinsing, in a single layer between paper towels and wrap in plastic.

To prepare cherries, rinse and stem them (**1**). Stone with a cherry stoner by pushing the plunger of the cherry stoner through the stem scar, stoning one by one into a small bowl (**2**).

Melon Soup

About 2 litres (3¼ pints)

Ripe cantaloupe and freshly squeezed juices are essential to this soup.
Purée in a food processor until smooth:

**2 medium very ripe and
sweet cantaloupes or other
orange-fleshed melons, peeled,
seeded, and cut into chunks**

Pour into a large bowl and stir in:
250ml (8floz) fresh orange juice
60ml (2floz) fresh lime juice
2 tbsp fresh lemon juice
Refrigerate until cold, about 2 hours.
When ready to serve, prepare:
**4 tbsp freshly grated
peeled ginger**

Using a muslin cloth or your hands, squeeze out the ginger juice into a small bowl. Stir 4 tsp of the juice into the soup. Serve in chilled bowls, garnished with:
**Thinly sliced kiwi fruit or
strawberries**
Fresh mint sprigs

Fruit Soup

About 1.5 litres (2½ pints)

In many Scandinavian homes, this soup is set out on the buffet table. It is good hot or cold.
Combine in a large saucepan and let stand for 45 minutes:

**125g (4oz) dried apricots or
peaches, quartered**
**140g (4½ oz) dried prunes, stoned
and quartered**
3 tbsp raisins
2 tbsp currants

Two 7.5cm (3in) cinnamon sticks
Grated zest of 1 orange
3 tbsp quick-cooking tapioca
**1 litre (1½ pints) apple juice,
cranberry juice or water**
Stir in:
4 tbsp of sugar
Bring to a boil, reduce the heat to low and simmer, stirring occasionally, until the fruit is softened and the soup is thickened,

about 30 minutes. Stir in:
**2 red apples, peeled, cored and cut
into 2.5cm (1in) pieces**
Cook until the apples are tender, about 8 minutes. Let cool and remove the cinnamon sticks. Serve warm or cold, garnished with:
**Crème fraîche, sour cream
or double cream**

DRIED FRUITS

The high caloric and nutritive values of dried fruits can be readily grasped if you consider that it takes 2.75kg (5½ lb) fresh apricots to yield 500g (1lb) dried. The fruits are suddenly not so expensive when you realize that there is no waste except the stones and that you are getting concentrated food value. When selecting dried fruits, look for the biggest and brightest, the plumpest, and those with uniform colour. Avoid fruits with blemishes and packets containing pieces of stalk or damaged fruits. Check for unnecessary additives. When a new box or packet is opened, do not store the fruits in the opened container. Dried fruits should be stored in tightly covered glass containers in a cool (7°-10°C/45°-50°F), dark, dry place or the refrigerator. Glass means you can see if any moisture is collecting inside, which will cause dry foods to spoil. All varieties must be watched for insects. Store far from foods like onions and garlic, because the fruits readily absorb other odours. Should sugaring develop – crystals of sugar forming on the surface of the skin – you can dip the fruit in boiling water, drain and dry at once. A cool, dry atmosphere will stop this happening.

ABOUT
CONDIMENTS
& QUICK BREADS

*W*hereas condiments differ widely in what they contain and how they are used, each occupies the same location in the culinary firmament, somewhere between a single spice and a side dish to be eaten on its own. Condiments can spice up, cool down or add richness to soups and stews. Every cook should have a few good recipes for salsas, sauces and flavoured mayonnaises in their repertoire. Bringing them to table can make an ordinary soup or stew special.

Quick breads are easy to make and a busy person's "rabbit from a hat". Homemade hot biscuits, for instance, can transform the simplest soup or stew into a satisfying meal.

Clockwise from top: *Basic Rolled Biscuits, 122; Salsa Fresca, 118; Pistou, 120*

Condiments for Soups and Stews

The characteristics of condiments tend to shift over time, but they do share a few attributes. All are used to provide flavour for food; all contain more than a single ingredient; all can be made in advance and most can be stored for at least a day or two, often much longer; and all stand alone, created independently and therefore able to add their distinctive flavours to a range of different dishes. (This last characteristic distinguishes them from pan sauces, which draw much of their flavour from the browned bits left in the pan after cooking poultry or meat.)

Condiments possess qualities that make them particularly useful for today's cooks. Most of them are quick and easy to prepare, and their intense flavours can make even a plain soup or stew an interesting meal. Also, since the recipes for condiments are flexible, a cook can adjust the flavour by adding more or less garlic, chilli pepper, vinegar, spices, lime juice and so on, depending on personal preference and on what the condiment will accompany. Serve these condiments as a garnish for soups or stews, or put them out on the table so your guests can help themselves.

Salsa Fresca

About 500ml (16floz)

This recipe for Mexican salsa is easily doubled or tripled, but make only as much as you will use immediately, as it loses its texture on standing and the chilli peppers increase in heat. Regional variations of salsa fresca include using spring onions or white or red onions, water instead of lime juice, and in Yucatán, sour-orange juice instead of lime juice. Precise amounts are less important than the happy marriage of flavours, so taste as you go.

Combine in a medium bowl:
½ small white or red onion or 8 slender spring onions, finely chopped, rinsed, and drained
2 tbsp fresh lime juice or cold water
Prepare the following ingredients, setting them aside, then add all together to the onion mixture:
2 large ripe tomatoes, or 3-5 ripe plum tomatoes, seeded, if desired, and finely diced
7-15g (¼ - ½ oz) chopped fresh coriander (leaves and tender stems)
3-5 serrano or fresh jalapeño peppers, or ¼ to 1 habanero pepper, or to taste, seeded and chopped
6 radishes, finely diced (optional)
1 medium clove garlic, finely chopped (optional)
Stir together well. Season with:
¼ tsp salt, or to taste
Serve immediately.

Garlic Mayonnaise (Aïoli)

About 250ml (8floz)

Sometimes called beurre de Provence *– the butter of Provence – aïoli is traditionally served slightly chilled as a sauce for cold poached fish, vegetables, meat or eggs. It also makes a luxurious garnish for hot and cold soups. Aïoli is a contraction of the Provençal words for garlic and oil.*
Whisk together in a medium bowl until smooth and light:

2 large egg yolks
4-6 cloves garlic, finely chopped
Salt and ground white pepper to taste
Whisk in by drops until the mixture starts to thicken and stiffen:
250ml (8floz) olive oil, or part olive and part safflower or peanut oil, at room temperature

As the sauce begins to thicken, whisk in the oil more steadily, making sure each addition is thoroughly blended before adding the next. Gradually whisk in:
1 tsp fresh lemon juice, or to taste
½ tsp cold water
Taste and adjust the seasonings. Serve immediately or refrigerate in a jar for 1 to 2 days.

Roast Tomato-Jalapeño Salsa

About 500ml (16floz)

Heat the grill. Arrange on a rimmed baking tray:

500g (1lb) red, ripe tomatoes

Grill 10cm (4in) from the heat until they blister, darken and soften on one side, about 4 minutes; turn them over and grill the other side until blistered and darkened, 5 to 6 minutes. Meanwhile, heat a dry cast-iron griddle or frying pan over high heat, and add:

2 large fresh jalapeño chilli peppers
3 cloves garlic, unpeeled

Shake them in the pan until their skins are soft and charred here and there, 5 to 10 minutes for the jalapeños, about 15 minutes for the garlic. Let cool, then peel the tomatoes, reserving the juices, pull the stems off the jalapeños and peel the garlic. Place the jalapeños and garlic in a food processor or blender with:

¼ tsp salt

Process to a coarse paste. Add the tomatoes and process a few times until you have a coarse-textured purée. Stir in:

½ small white onion, finely
   chopped, rinsed and drained
Generous 5 tbsp chopped fresh
   coriander
About 1½ tsp cider vinegar
   (optional)

Add 2 to 4 tbsp water, if necessary, to give the salsa a fairly thick but easily spoonable consistency. Taste and season with:

Salt

Serve immediately.

JALAPEÑO PEPPER

These stubby green to red chillies are widely available and can vary considerably in their heat from totally mild (a new heatless jalapeño is now being grown for use in commercial salsa) to quite hot varieties found in farmers' markets and their homeland of Veracruz, Mexico. The jalapeño pepper's bright green, juicy, grassy taste works well in many dishes, from raw salsas to soups and stews. This pepper is also good stuffed and fried. When mature jalapeños are smoked and dried, they are known as chipotles. Fresh jalapeños measure about 6cm (2½ in) long and 2cm (¾ in) wide at the stem end and taper a little before coming to a rather blunt tip.

Saffron Garlic Mayonnaise (Rouille)

About 250ml (8floz)

This thick, garlicky, bright-gold sauce is the essential finish for Bouillabaisse, 86, and other Provençal fish soups and stews. It is also wonderful with fish, seafood, meats, poultry and vegetables from the oven or barbecue. All rouilles are brilliant in colour. Some cooks use puréed roast red peppers, but we vote for saffron.

Stir together in a small bowl, cover, and let stand for 10 minutes:

¾ tsp saffron threads, or
   ⅛ tsp powdered saffron
2 tbsp hot stock from the soup to
   be garnished, or water

Process in a food processor to fine crumbs:

1 fresh French roll (not
   sourdough), crust trimmed

Add 60g (2oz) of the breadcrumbs to the saffron infusion. Mash with a fork to a loose paste, stirring in, if necessary:

Up to 1 tbsp hot stock or water

Place in a mortar or small bowl:

1 large dried red chilli pepper,
   seeded

Vigorously pound to a powder with a pestle or sturdy wooden spoon. Add and pound until the garlic is puréed:

3 small cloves garlic, peeled
⅛ tsp coarse salt

Stir in:

1 large egg yolk

Stir in the bread paste bit by bit, then work vigorously until blended and smooth. Whisk in by drops until the mixture starts to thicken and stiffen:

About 180ml (6floz) olive oil, or
   part olive and part safflower oil,
   at room temperature

Let the oil fall to one side of the mortar or bowl, very slowly at first, while you stir it in without stopping. (If the sauce should start to curdle, simply stir in a little hot stock or water.) When the mixture has absorbed all the oil it can, season with:

Salt to taste

Cover and refrigerate. Use the same day.

Pistou

About 250ml (8floz)

The Provençal version of Italy's pesto, made without nuts, makes a great addition to soups and stews.

Vigorously pound to a paste with a pestle and mortar, or process in a food processor or blender until the garlic is finely chopped:

4-6 large cloves garlic, peeled
Pinch of coarse salt

Gradually add and pound, or process, to a dark green paste:

75g (2½ oz) fresh basil leaves

Add in 4 batches and pound, or pulse, to the consistency of soft butter:

45g (1½ oz) grated Parmesan or Gruyère cheese

Gradually add and pound, or with the machine running, pour through the feed tube in a slow, steady stream, until the sauce has the consistency of coarse mayonnaise:

80ml (3floz) olive oil, preferably extra-virgin

Season with:

Salt and ground black pepper to taste

Serve at room temperature or store, covered and refrigerated, for up to 2 days.

Avgolemono

About 300ml (½ pint)

This favourite Greek sauce is good with soups and stews – anything, say the Greeks, that is not made with garlic or tomatoes.

Stir together in a small bowl:

1 tbsp cold water
1 tsp cornflour

Whisk together in a small, heavy stainless-steel saucepan over low heat just until warm:

3 large egg yolks
3-4 tbsp fresh lemon juice

Pour the cornflour mixture into the egg mixture. Gradually add, stirring or whisking constantly:

250ml (8floz) *Vegetable Stock, 20, or Express Chicken Broth, 29*

Cook, stirring constantly, over medium-low heat until thick and creamy and the sauce coats the back of a spoon; do not let the sauce get too hot, or the eggs will curdle. Remove the sauce from the heat and stir in:

Salt and ground black pepper to taste

Serve immediately.

Nam Prik (Thai Hot Sauce)

About 160ml (5floz)

Nam prik, which translates as "pepper water", is the traditional table sauce of Thailand. It is stirred into soups, as well as used to season rice, noodles or vegetables. The sauce is best a day or two after making, and keeps well in the refrigerator. If dried prawns and fish sauce are not available, add more fresh or dried chilli peppers and lime juice.

Pound to a paste with a pestle and mortar or process in a small food processor or blender:

18 tiny dried prawns, chopped
4 small dried red chilli peppers, seeded, if desired, and crumbled
4 cloves garlic, chopped
2 tbsp fresh lime juice

1 tbsp fish sauce
Stir in:
3 small red or green serrano peppers, seeded, if desired, and finely chopped
Chopped fresh coriander to taste
A little brown sugar (optional)
Cover and refrigerate for at least 1 day before serving.

Chilli Oil

About 180ml (6floz)

This oil is exceedingly hot – use sparingly. A few drops are superb in Oriental soups. Although there are many different peppers in Oriental supermarkets labelled "Thai peppers", perhaps the most common in this country are the small, elongated, pointy green to red peppers sold with their stems attached. These intensely hot peppers measure about 4cm (1½ in) long and only 5mm (¼ in) wide.

Coarsely chop in a blender or spice grinder:

45g (1½ oz) dried chilli peppers, preferably Thai

Transfer to a stainless-steel saucepan and add:

180ml (6floz) peanut oil

Cook over medium heat until the peppers begin to foam. Remove from the heat when some of the smallest flecks on the side of the pan blacken. Cover, and let sit for 4 to 6 hours. Strain through a dampened paper coffee filter into a scrupulously clean jar or bottle. This keeps, covered and refrigerated, for up to 1 month.

Harissa

About 80ml (3floz)

In North Africa, this fiery pepper paste is stirred into soups and seafood stews.
Combine in a small dry frying pan over medium heat and toast, shaking the pan often to prevent burning, until very aromatic, 2 to 3 minutes:

1 tsp caraway seeds
1 tsp coriander seeds
½ tsp cumin seeds

Remove from the heat, let cool to room temperature and grind to a fine powder in a spice grinder, coffee grinder, blender, or with a pestle and mortar. Add and grind again until smooth:

2 cloves garlic, quartered
Salt to taste
Add and grind until all the ingredients are well combined:
3 tbsp sweet paprika
1 tbsp crushed chilli flakes
1 tbsp olive oil
The harissa will be very thick and dry. Transfer the paste to a small jar and cover with:
Olive oil
Store, covered, in the refrigerator; it will keep for 6 months.

PAPRIKA

Finely ground dried ripe peppers constitute this spice. Depending on the pepper used, the colour varies from light orange to deep red, the flavour from bland to rich but mild. *Sweet* paprika is ground from the flesh of particularly sweet peppers with most, if not all, of their seeds and ribs removed – these parts can be sharp tasting. The best paprika has long come from Hungary, where paprika making is an important culinary tradition.

Breads for Serving with Soups and Stews

Quick breads are so called because they are quickly mixed and, with the absence of yeast, need no lengthy rising time before baking. Thus gratification is never delayed. These breads encompass muffins, corn breads and savoury loaves to serve with soups and stews.

Americans serve a cross between a muffin and a scone, which they call "biscuit", with soups and stews. Made in the same way as a scone, they can either be served in the stew or as an accompaniment. A survey of good biscuit recipes proves that they are quite forgiving. Some cooks use twice the amount of baking powder. Some use four times the amount of butter. Even the size of the fat pieces cut into the flour varies. Nor is there a precise proportion of liquid to flour, for good rolled biscuits seem to be made from both fairly stiff and soft doughs.

Corn bread, a hearty quick bread made with coarse meal, is well suited to serving with soups and stews. Americans from the south who grew up on corn bread know the hanker-ing for its rich brown crust, crunchy edges and slightly gritty bite. The ultimate southern experience demands both stone-ground meal *and* a preheated heavy pan to supply the required crustiness. The cakier northern soft corn bread also reaches its pinnacle with stone-ground meal.

Like corn bread, other savoury quick breads are made from simple batters that can be studded with all kinds of ingredients – from olives and nuts to bacon and cheese.

Basic Rolled Biscuits

Twenty 5cm (2in) biscuits

You can shape and cut essentially any shape you like with this dough. These biscuits go nicely alongside a hearty stew or flavourful soup.

Position a rack in the centre of the oven. Preheat the oven to 230°C (450°F) Gas 8. Have ready a large ungreased baking tray.
Whisk together thoroughly in a large bowl:

315g (10oz) plain flour
2½ tsp baking powder
½ - ¾ tsp salt
Drop in:
75-90g (2½-3oz) cold unsalted butter, cut into pieces
Cut in the butter with 2 knives or a pastry blender, tossing the pieces with the flour mixture to coat and separate them as you work. For biscuits with crunchy edges and a flaky, layered structure, continue to cut in the butter until the largest pieces are the size of peas and the rest resemble breadcrumbs. For classic fluffy biscuits, continue to cut in the butter until the mixture resembles coarse breadcrumbs. Do not allow the butter to melt or form a paste with the flour.
Add all at once:
180ml (6floz) milk
Mix with a rubber spatula, wooden spoon or fork just until most of the dry ingredients are moistened. With a lightly floured hand, gather the dough into a ball and knead it gently against the sides and bottom of the bowl 5 to 10 times, turning and pressing any loose pieces into the dough each time until they adhere and the bowl is fairly clean.
To shape round biscuits: transfer the dough to a lightly floured sur-face. With a lightly floured rolling pin or your fingers, roll out or pat the dough 1cm (½ in) thick. Cut out 4.5-5cm (1¾-2in) rounds with a drinking glass or biscuit cutter dipped in flour; push the cutter straight down into the dough and pull it out without twisting for biscuits that will rise evenly. You can reroll the scraps and cut additional biscuits.
To shape square biscuits (with virtually no scraps): roll out the dough 1cm (½ in) thick (5mm-1cm/ ¼ - ⅜ in if cooking on a griddle) into a square or rectangle. Trim a fraction of dough from the edges with a sharp knife before cutting into 5cm (2in) squares.
For browner tops, you can brush the biscuit tops with:
Milk or melted butter
Place the biscuits on a baking tray at least 2.5cm (1in) apart for biscuits with crusty sides or close together for biscuits that are joined and remain soft on the sides. Bake until the biscuits are golden brown on the top and a deeper golden brown on the bottom, 10 to 12 minutes. Serve hot.

Cream Biscuits

Twenty 5cm (2in) biscuits

Position a rack in the centre of the oven. Preheat the oven to 230°C (450°F) Gas 8. Have ready a large ungreased baking tray.
Whisk together thoroughly in a large bowl:

315g (10oz) plain flour
2½ tsp baking powder
½ - ¾ tsp salt

Add all at once:
300ml (10floz) double cream
Mix with a rubber spatula, wooden spoon or fork just until most of the dry ingredients are moistened. Knead, shape and bake as directed for *Basic Rolled Biscuits, opposite.*
Serve hot.

American Corn Bread

8 servings

Real southern American corn bread is made only with stone-ground cornmeal (tradition dictates white), buttermilk, eggs, leavening and salt – no flour and no sugar. Some southern cooks stir in a tablespoon of bacon fat.

Position a rack in the upper third of the oven. Preheat the oven to 230°C (450°F) Gas 8. Place in a heavy 23cm (9in) frying pan, preferably cast-iron, or less ideally, a 20 x 20cm (8 x 8in) glass baking dish:

1 tbsp bacon fat, lard or vegetable lard

Whisk together thoroughly in a large bowl:

220g (7oz) stone-ground cornmeal, preferably white
1 tbsp sugar (optional)
1 tsp baking powder
1 tsp bicarbonate of soda
1 tsp salt (¾ tsp if using buttermilk with salt)

Whisk until foamy in another bowl:
2 large eggs
Whisk in:
500ml (16floz) buttermilk
Add the wet ingredients to the dry ingredients and whisk just until blended. Place the frying pan or dish

in the oven and heat until the fat smokes. Pour in the batter all at once. Bake until the top is browned and the centre feels firm when pressed, 20 to 25 minutes. Serve immediately from the pan, cut in wedges or squares, with:

Butter
Leftovers, though dry, are nice enough if wrapped in foil and rewarmed in a low oven.

CORN MUFFINS

Quick breads can be baked in any size pan with small adjustments to baking time. Use a corn muffin tin for these favourites.
Prepare *American Corn Bread, left.* Generously brush a corn muffin tin with oil or melted lard and heat in a preheated 230°C (450°F) Gas 8 oven until the fat smokes. Fill the cups two-thirds full. Bake for 10 to 15 minutes. Prise out onto a rack with a knife or fork. Brush out any crumbs, regrease and continue with the rest of the batter. The yield will vary depending on the tin you use.

Soft Corn Bread

10 to 12 servings

Here a mixture of cornmeal and flour and a combination of milk and buttermilk yield a lighter corn bread with a more cakey texture than American Corn Bread, 123.

Position a rack in the centre of the oven. Preheat the oven to 220°C (425°F) Gas 7. Grease a 23 x 23cm (9 x 9in) tin or a 12-muffin tin or line the muffin tin with paper cups. Whisk together in a large bowl:

155g (5oz) stone-ground cornmeal
125g (4oz) plain flour
1-4 tbsp sugar
2 tsp baking powder
½ tsp bicarbonate of soda
½ tsp salt

Whisk together in another bowl:

2 large eggs
160ml (5floz) milk
160ml (5floz) buttermilk

Add the wet ingredients to the dry ingredients and stir just until moistened. Fold in:

30-45g (1-1½oz) warm melted unsalted butter or vegetable oil

Scrape the batter into the tin and tilt (if using a square pan) to spread evenly. Bake until a toothpick inserted in the centre comes out clean, 10 to 12 minutes in a muffin tin, 20 to 25 minutes in a square tin. Serve hot.

Smoky Bacon, Cheese and Roasted Hot Pepper Corn Bread

Very spicy, robust and satisfying – possibly the best hot and spicy corn bread of them all.

Prepare and let cool:

2 fresh jalapeño peppers, roasted until the skins are blackened, skinned, seeded and diced
1 red pepper, roasted until the skin is blackened, skinned, seeded and diced
6 slices bacon, diced, fried until crisp, drained and blotted

Combine in a medium bowl and toss with:

60g (2oz) grated mature Cheddar cheese

Prepare *American Corn Bread, 123*, using 1 tbsp sugar and adding to the dry ingredients:

1 tbsp chilli powder

Fold the prepared pepper mixture into the completed batter.

MAKING CROUTONS

These dried or fried seasoned fresh bread morsels come in all sizes and are perfect for garnishing soups and stews. Croutons are made by cutting bread, preferably simple French bread, into small or large dice or square slices, buttering them or rubbing them with olive oil, and toasting in a 190°C (375°F) Gas 5 oven until crisp, 10 to 15 minutes.

Mediterranean Olive Bread

8 to 10 servings

Position a rack in the lower third of the oven. Preheat the oven to 180°C (350°F) Gas 4. Grease a 22 x 12cm (8½ x 4½ in) loaf tin. Whisk together thoroughly:

230g (7½oz) plain flour
140g (4½oz) wholemeal flour
2½ tsp baking powder
¾ tsp dried rosemary, or 1 tsp chopped fresh

½ tsp salt

Whisk together in a large bowl:

2 large eggs
250ml (8floz) milk
60ml (2floz) olive oil

Add the flour mixture and fold until about three-quarters of the dry ingredients are moistened. Add:

5 tbsp finely chopped walnuts
5 tbsp cup chopped stoned olives

Fold just until the pieces are distributed and the dry ingredients are moistened; the batter will be stiff. Scrape the batter into the tin and spread evenly. Bake until a toothpick inserted in the centre comes out clean, 40 to 45 minutes. Let cool in the tin on a rack for 5 to 10 minutes before unmoulding to cool completely on the rack.

Quick Beer Bread

8 servings

Serve with hearty soups or stews and cheeses. Slices are good toasted, or you can rewarm the whole loaf in the oven.

Position a rack in the lower third of the oven. Preheat the oven to 200°C (400°F) Gas 6. Grease a 22 x 12cm (8½ x 4½ in) loaf tin.

Whisk together thoroughly in a large bowl:

185g (6oz) wholemeal flour
155g (5oz) plain flour
45g (1½ oz) rolled oats
2 tbsp sugar
2 tsp baking powder
½ tsp bicarbonate of soda
½ tsp salt
Add:
375ml (12floz) beer (but not
stout), cold or at room
temperature but not flat

Fold just until the dry ingredients are moistened. Scrape the batter into the tin and spread evenly. Bake until a toothpick inserted in the centre and all the way to the bottom of the tin comes out clean, 35 to 40 minutes. Let cool in the tin on a rack for 5 to 10 minutes before unmoulding to cool completely on the rack.

Courgette Cheddar Bread

10 to 12 servings

We make this whether or not the garden runneth over! Serve with soup for lunch or with a hearty stew for dinner. This is lovely toasted the next day.

Position a rack in the centre of the oven. Preheat the oven to 180°C (350°F) Gas 4. Grease a 23 x 13cm (9 x 5in) loaf tin.

Whisk together thoroughly in a large bowl:

500g (1lb) plain flour
4 tsp baking powder
1 tsp salt
½ tsp bicarbonate of soda
Add and toss to separate and coat with flour:
90g (3oz) coarsely grated courgette
60g (2oz) grated mature
Cheddar cheese
4 tbsp chopped spring onions
3 tbsp chopped fresh parsley
1 tbsp snipped fresh dill, or
2 tsp dried
Whisk together in another bowl:
2 large eggs
250ml (8floz) buttermilk
60g (2oz) warm melted unsalted
butter or 4 tbsp vegetable oil

Add to the flour mixture and mix with a few light strokes just until the dry ingredients are moistened. Do not overmix; the batter should not be smooth. Bake until a toothpick inserted in the centre comes out clean, 55 to 60 minutes. Let cool in the tin on a rack for 5 to 10 minutes before unmoulding to cool completely on the rack.

COURGETTES

Courgettes, perhaps the best known summer squash, are thin, dark green and 15-20cm (6-8in) long. Select the smallest, firmest, glossiest courgettes, heaviest for their size, without soft spots or other blemishes. Store in perforated plastic vegetable bags in the refrigerator drawer. With their mild, sweet flesh, courgettes are excellent with most of summer's harvest, especially tomatoes, onions, peppers (both sweet and chilli), garlic, oregano, marjoram, basil, parsley, dill, rosemary, olive oil and capers. Sometimes, you will find courgettes with blossoms still attached. They are delightful stuffed and baked, and they make lovely sweet or savoury fritters. Squash blossoms are delicate and should be prepared on the same day as purchase. Keep them in the refrigerator drawer until ready to use.

Index

Bold type indicates that a recipe has an accompanying photograph.

ACKNOWLEDGEMENTS

Special thanks to my wife and editor in residence, Susan; our indispensable assistant and comrade, Mary Gilbert; and our friends and agents, Gene Winick and Sam Pinkus. Much appreciation also goes to Simon & Schuster, Scribner and Weldon Owen for their devotion to this project. Thank you Carolyn, Susan, Bill, Marah, John, Terry, Roger, Gaye, Val, Norman and all the other capable and talented folks who gave a part of themselves to the Joy of Cooking All About series.

My eternal appreciation goes to the food experts, writers and editors whose contributions and collaborations are at the heart of Joy – especially Stephen Schmidt. He was to the 1997 edition what Chef Pierre Adrian was to Mom's final editions of Joy. Thank you one and all.

Ethan Becker

FOOD EXPERTS, WRITERS AND EDITORS

Selma Abrams, Jody Adams, Samia Ahad, Bruce Aidells, Katherine Alford, Deirdre Allen, Pam Anderson, Elizabeth Andoh, Phillip Andres, Alice Arndt, John Ash, Nancy Baggett, Rick and Deann Bayless, Lee E. Benning, Rose Levy Beranbaum, Brigit Legere Binns, Jack Bishop, Carole Bloom, Arthur Boehm, Ed Brown, JeanMarie Brownson, Larry Catanzaro, Val Cipollone, Polly Clingerman, Elaine Corn, Bruce Cost, Amy Cotler, Brian Crawley, Gail Damerow, Linda Dann, Deirdre Davis, Jane Spencer Davis, Erica De Mane, Susan Derecskey, Abigail Johnson Dodge, Jim Dodge, Aurora Esther, Michele Fagerroos, Eva Forson, Margaret Fox, Betty Fussell, Mary Gilbert, Darra Goldstein, Elaine Gonzalez, Dorie Greenspan, Maria Guarnaschelli, Helen Gustafson, Pat Haley, Gordon Hamersley, Melissa Hamilton, Jessica Harris, Hallie Harron, Nao Hauser, William Hay, Larry Hayden, Kate Hays, Marcella Hazan, Tim Healea, Janie Hibler, Lee Hofstetter, Paula Hogan, Rosemary Howe, Mike Hughes, Jennifer Humphries, Dana Jacobi, Stephen Johnson, Lynne Rossetto Kasper, Denis Kelly, Fran Kennedy, Johanne Killeen and George Germon, Shirley King, Maya Klein, Diane M. Kochilas, Phyllis Kohn, Aglaia Kremezi, Mildred Kroll, Loni Kuhn, Corby Kummer, Virginia Lawrence, Jill Leigh, Karen Levin, Lori Longbotham, Susan Hermann Loomis, Emily Luchetti, Stephanie Lyness, Karen MacNeil, Deborah Madison, Linda Marino, Kathleen McAndrews, Alice Medrich, Anne Mendelson, Lisa Montenegro, Cindy Mushet, Marion Nestle, Toby Oksman, Joyce O'Neill, Suzen O'Rourke, Russ Parsons, Holly Pearson, James Peterson, Marina Petrakos, Mary Placek, Maricel Presilla, Marion K. Pruitt, Adam Rapoport, Mardee Haidin Regan, Peter Reinhart, Sarah Anne Reynolds, Madge Rosenberg, Nicole Routhier, Jon Rowley, Nancy Ross Ryan, Chris Schlesinger, Stephen Schmidt, Lisa Schumacher, Marie Simmons, Nina Simonds, A. Cort Sinnes, Sue Spitler, Marah Stets, Molly Stevens, Christopher Stoye, Susan Stuck, Sylvia Thompson, Jean and Pierre Troisgros, Jill Van Cleave, Patricia Wells, Laurie Wenk, Caroline Wheaton, Jasper White, Jonathan White, Marilyn Wilkenson, Carla Williams, Virginia Willis, John Willoughby, Deborah Winson, Lisa Yockelson.

Weldon Owen wishes to thank the following people for their generous assistance and support in producing this book: Desne Border, Ken DellaPenta and Joan Olson.